NOTES FROM THE
END OF EVERYTHING

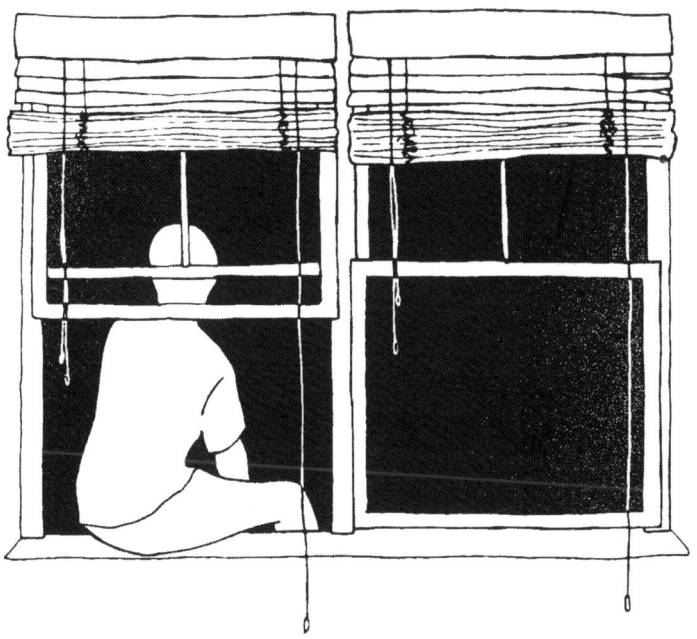

ROBERT PANTANO
of Pursuit of Wonder

CONTENTS

INTRODUCTION

John Gallo was an American author most popularly known for his two novels *The Tragedy of Good Luck* and *A Reason to Stop Worrying*. Throughout his life, he published seven novels and three short story collections. His work was often marked by broad philosophical themes, exploring concepts such as human meaning, connection, nature, chaos, and conflicts between perception and reality.

In 2014, Gallo was diagnosed with a brain tumor, which soon after was found to be malignant. He wrote on and off during this time, producing a collection of fragmentary journal-like essays on his ruminations of life, death, and anything in between.

The collection was found on his laptop, saved as the only file on his desktop. The file was titled *Notes from the End of Everything*.

At the careful discretion of close family, friends, and colleagues, some of the original work has been removed, slightly edited, and pieced together (mostly towards the end) in order to help assist the comprehension of Gallo's declining mind as the effects of his tumor and cancer treatments worsened.

This is the condensed, curated version of that work.

CHAPTER 1:
FINDING OUT YOU'RE GOING TO DIE

1

You never truly know the good news from the bad until you receive your last piece of bad news ever.

I have lived knowing that, at any moment, everything could fall apart or end; but of course, knowing this is never the same as actually confronting it.

I could tell it was bad news before he even said anything. The intricate, minute details of his body language and facial gestures created a weight in the room that I could feel subconsciously. Each moment observing him drew the feeling further and further out of the realm of abstract sense and into conscious certainty. I could see my fate in his forced widened eyes. I could see my life shortening.

2

Being born renders two inevitable experiences: living and dying. And both are terrifying.

Throughout my life, I've worried about dying. It wasn't always a conscious worry. Sometimes it was. But sometimes it just existed as a buzzing in the background that revealed itself when I heard weird noises late at night. Or when I felt a strange pain behind the ear on the left side of my skull. Or when I was on a plane or in the subway or in a crowd and something just seemed off, even if it was just my mood.

In any number of these common moments, I was reminded, at least subconsciously, that the only thing keeping everything from nothing is just a fragile shell holding in some liquid and paste. And outside that shell is chaos; a hellfire of cosmic phenomena flying around, indifferent to my existence. And frankly, inside is not much better. Essentially, anything outside of the voice that is writing this—from the stars and trees and other human beings outside my window, to the microbial germs and bacteria inside my body—all is a warzone of objects and materials constantly on the fringe of peace and chaos. And I am in the middle of it. We are all in the middle of it.

This warzone isn't even something to complain about. I don't claim to know whether it is a good or bad thing. But it is clear that it can be terrifying.

Ironically, that feeling behind the ear on the left side of my skull wasn't like when I mistook the furnace kicking on for someone trying to break into my house. Or like that heavy bump on a plane that ends up just being regular turbulence. It was a tumor.

It was, is, an astrocytoma, which is a brain tumor of the glioma type. The doctor told me around a week ago that my brain scan tests revealed it in the back section of my cerebrum.

About three or four weeks prior, that pain on the back of my head had become increasingly worse, developing into a horrible, consistent headache. After a while of trying to avoid dealing with it and hoping it would just go away, I saw my primary care doctor who, after being unable to diagnose it himself, referred me to a neurologist who administered some tests and brain scans and eventually, a week or so later, revealed my fate.

He said it was too early to tell for sure what's going on, how fast it's growing, if it's definitely cancerous, what grade it is, and how treatments could help remove or mitigate it. But it appeared to be quite big and showing signs of malignancy. He didn't explicitly say I shouldn't get my hopes up, but based on his tone and careful choice of words, I understood.

He said that generally, if the tumor is benign, it can be plucked out with one or more surgeries and the patient can return to life as normal. But if it's malignant, depending on the type and degree, it can get rather complicated. He explained the severity and time sensitive nature of what was happening and then explained what he believed should happen next.

I'm going back in for more tests in two days to find out whether a biopsy will be necessary to determine the grade of the tumor.

I spent the entire night and days following the diagnostic appointment researching tumors online. It would seem that if it's not benign, I have somewhere around a 50 percent chance of living past five years. That's best case. But a tumor of substantial size, which mine is, and one that is aggressively malignant, which mine might be, can potentially bring that median survival rate down closer to twelve to eighteen months with only about a 5 percent chance of living past five years.

With surgeries, chemotherapy, radiation treatments, and other methods and drugs, it's possible to bump that back up. Potentially closer to three or five plus years, even with an otherwise aggressive tumor. But in truth, if you really did all the arithmetic and accounted for all the potential variances of factors and risks and complexities, it would probably still be closer to one at best. This is all to say that I could likely be looking at one more year.

3

The further tests and MRI scans weren't clear enough to diagnose the tumor. I had a biopsy two days later, now about five days ago. They went into my skull to take a part of the brain tumor out and examine it under a microscope.

It's now been conclusively diagnosed as malignant. A grade 3 astrocytoma is the current, official diagnosis, which is somewhere in the middle of worst-case scenario. Almost certainly fatal. I say almost only because I haven't really come to terms with just saying certainly yet.

4

For the first time, I am no longer curious about how I am going to die. Now I know. And for the first time, I've felt a little peace in the thought of my death. Not peace with dying, but peace in the knowledge of how and when. It's like someone had told me that, when I least expected it, they were going to punch me. I've been on the edge anticipating the punch my whole life and now they finally hit me. It hurts so fucking much, but I am no longer worried about when or how it's going to happen.

Of course, it's a lot sooner than I was expecting. And hoping. But I'm not sure how much of a difference this really makes. I don't know if there would ever be a time in which I would be ready to die. At least no more or less than I am now.

If this wasn't all happening—if I was looking at another fifty years instead of two or three—I'd either age into a tired, old man, ready to die, or age into a tired, old man who isn't. Both would be equally miserable and sad.

If you're ready for death, it's because life has already killed you. If you're not ready for death, death will either kill you before you are, or you'll eventually be ready for death and be the same as the first option. At some point, you either lose your life while you're alive or you lose it by death. And no one is ever ready for or happy with either.

I would argue that, after a certain point, it doesn't matter all that much how long someone lives. My life is ending short only because of my view of what constitutes *long* or *full*. The length of one's life is, like all things, relative to what it's being measured against. If it were measured against a second in time, my life has already lasted as long as some of the stars; but if measured against the stars, even if I lived for another thousand years, my life would be a flash of inconsequential nothingness.

No matter how long one lives, one always perceives their life's length against their expectations of its length, not any objective measurement. And thus, one's length of life is not even a viable, objective measurement of one's experience of it.

A greater length does not imply greater depth. If a person had the option to live fifteen years of immense vigor and luster or one hundred years of suffering tedium, wouldn't the fairly obvious choice be the fifteen good years over the one hundred bad? In truth, someone dying earlier than expected could be just as sad as someone dying as expected but living an arduous, horrible life.

And so, what does this suggest about my diagnosis and young death? It's sad, sure, but perhaps no more or less than any other way this whole thing could have gone.

Am I ready to die? I don't know. Does it matter? No.

5

In the movies, someone in my position might travel, pick up new passions, chase lusts and sexual fantasies, find new loves, or change in some dramatic, grandiose way.

But I choose to spend my time mostly how I always have. I see friends and family I'm close with, go on walks around the neighborhood and on local forest trails and in the neighboring city, drink good whiskey and eat at my favorite places, enjoy TV shows, films, books, and this, right now: writing.

I obviously can't say for sure, but I think I'll probably just continue spending my time on these same things; the things I mostly always have. There's not much else to do.

I've written most of my adult life. Both personally and professionally. I was never really a fan of writing when I was a child or young teenager, but I was always into talking, storytelling, arguing, and reasoning, which was perhaps a sign of an innate interest in writing in some form or another.

The interest really started to surface in my late teens and early twenties. Stuff I wrote in high school and college began to get noticed by teachers and professors. And when enough people start noticing and suggesting the quality of your work, eventually you start to believe them. You start to associate yourself with the thing and lean further in its direction. As I grew older, I began to subsume writing more as a potential part of my identity and direction in life, befriending other people with similar, basic literary interests, and working towards turning writing into a living.

I found a certain interest and passion for writing during my early twenties. A feeling that I had only really felt one or two other times as a much younger child for the sort of classic young-boy sports obsessions, which naturally waned with age. I rediscovered that same sort of passionate, youthful obsession in writing. And I don't imagine you get many of those in a lifetime, so I followed it.

I wrote my first real book when I was twenty-two, which I submitted as my undergraduate English thesis at Umass Boston. With some additional help and nudging from a professor, and after a lot of rejection, I eventually got it published. It didn't do that well. But well enough. Well enough to pay me a little and keep me writing.

During my early and mid-twenties, I worked a mix of horrible, but standard post-graduate jobs while writing along the side. At about twenty-six, I published *The Tragedy of Good Luck*, which the following year went on to become quite popular.

I haven't stopped since. I've written about 9 or so more books. Some good. Some great. Some not so good or great. But overall, I've done alright.

I suppose it says something about how I chose to spend my time if, in the thralls of my waning life, I choose to do the same thing. Or perhaps it merely suggests that I've formed the habit of writing and don't know how to do anything else with my time. I prefer to believe the former.

Typically, I write fiction. But mostly because I find that creating fake worlds and lives helps me better express my own. That's the trick to good writing, I think; to trick yourself into being honest with yourself. However, now I don't feel so much of a need to do that. I feel as though my thoughts—my voice—they should stand on their own in their own world while they still can.

With my mortality inescapably closer, there is not enough future to escape to. And so now I feel as though there is nothing to wait for. Nothing to conceal or hide. I will just write whatever I think whenever I feel like writing until I can't write or think anymore.

The irony is that I needed a brain tumor to finally do that.

6

I know that I know no more than anyone else in the general, existential sense. But by the same token, I know no less in the general, existential sense. I simply seek to share how I feel and say what I've experienced while I still have a brain to experience and a voice to speak.

If my philosophies and takes on life seem to have any similarities or redundancies to anyone else who has come before or next to me, it is because they probably do. I don't pretend that any idea, thought, or line here is new, old, unique, trite, or anywhere in between. I have no idea. Even this sentiment carries some staleness. Ultimately, we have all lived through the same basic form of life, and thus, those who make it their business to pay close, rational attention likely notice similar patterns. And thus, some similar forms of *wisdom* and *philosophy* might naturally emerge.

Furthermore, I have spent much of my life listening, reading, and learning from others, drawn to those who I have felt an affinity towards and pushed away from those who I have not. How can one find their own voice except in some combination of the voices of others? And perhaps mostly everything anyone says is, at some point, mostly the same, but just in different orders of different words.

Arguably, to some extent, all voices are but amalgamations of the voices one has heard, liked, and hated. The true test of a voice is how well one fends for their unique amalgamation. How well one assembles their perceptions and absorptions into a singular, unique, artful output. How successful I am at this is not mine to decide, but it is mine to try and defend.

I have no interest in new or old ideas; I have interest in what I find to be properly agreeable and fair in my particular defense and conveyance of it. But on that same note, if what I write is foolish or absurd, it is because it probably is. It is because everything probably is. Language and thought are but absurd abstractions of an already absurd and abstract reality. And everything said, written, and lived is bound up in it.

I write now, in my final time, for the same reason I wrote when I started writing. I write because it feels like there's a lot to say and no way to say it. Or, for some reason, it feels like there's a lot to say about how little there is to say. Or perhaps because the blank page is the only thing that will listen long enough for me to make any sense of this confusing senselessness.

In me, like everyone else, there is an insatiable yearning to share and be shared with in a world filled with hidden souls. To be understood from inside a brain that is impossible to understand. To grasp at truth in a reality that constantly changes it. To squeeze out any remaining life still bottled in my head in the futile attempt to make it worth something.

And so, I write.

CHAPTER 2:
WELL WASTED TIME

7

My doctor said I will be needing surgery as soon as possible to try and reduce the tumor's size. He told me that multiple surgeries might be necessary and the sooner they can get in and start, the better.

Surgeries and treatments are the difference between what could be less than several months and more than a couple years left. It's also possible that with certain treatments and surgeries, it could be even more than a couple years. But that seems a lot more like an "anything is possible" type of notion rather than a real one.

At this point, it's still unclear how much can be taken out and how effective it will even be.

The problem with tumors, it seems, is that they're smart. Of course, they're not smart in the conscious way, but they seem to have what I would liken to an instinctual cleverness in getting what they want. An aptitude towards their goals paired with an ability to adapt and circumvent whatever attempts to get in their way. Almost like how a lion hunting a gazelle might juke one way and then run the other. Or perhaps the gazelle might. In either case, that's sort of what I'm up against.

I scheduled a surgery in a little more than a week. Despite the obvious risks, I figure anything is better than nothing and I'm willing to wager a little for a little more.

8

At birth, I was given three hundred and sixty-five days a year and, at best, about eighty to one hundred or so years. Obviously, things are not always at best. In any case, the funny thing about viscerally realizing that you likely have this many days and years is that when you do, and you really become aware of what having days and years means, it makes it harder to spend them well.

When you're young, you don't realize how precious time is. When you're old, you know how precious it is, but don't know how to enjoy it the same anymore.

Time is the most valuable thing. That's what people say. This seems undisputable on the surface, I suppose; but fundamentally, I don't know if time is inherently any more valuable than anything else. With no one to spend it, time means nothing. Time is no different than money in this sense. It is only valuable when spent on something deemed personally valuable by the spender. Otherwise, it's merely conceptual. No one can spend their time on more time, just like no one can principally buy more than a dollar bill with another dollar bill. A dollar is only worth what someone buys with it other than itself. Likewise, time is only as valuable as what one spends it on other than itself.

The distinct and obvious difference is that we are all born with our potential quantities of time. It's our intrinsic birthright gift: a lump sum of time. However, also distinct to time, we have to spend it every second. We can't save it. We can't acquire more than the amount we're *given*. We can't do anything with it other than spend it—even before we realize we have it. And when we realize we're spending it, we continue to spend it rashly, every moment forcing us to spend more of itself on itself. We can't even spend time trying to determine how we want to spend time without spending time. And in this, the pressure of wasting time never alleviates. We are born into it and thrown through it. There is no moment to properly stop and evaluate time from outside time itself.

To properly spend one's time, one needs enough time to evaluate time properly. To try as many things, go through as many different processes, experience different lifestyles, visit different places, live with different people, and so on. But there is not even close to enough time to do a fraction of any of this. And so we all meander through our absurd lives, filling our time with endeavors, pursuits, and activities, not because we know that it's what we want to do, nor what we should do, but because we have time and it must be spent.

9

The surgery was successful. At least in terms of not killing me. They were able to take a relatively decent amount of the tumor out, but the problem, which became clearer once inside, is that the tumor appeared to be showing initial signs of insidious growth. In other words, it's not growing like a single mass or ball-shaped tumor, but rather, it's starting to slightly feather or wing out like a map or butterfly. This essentially makes it impossible to take the whole thing out. And it's also rather horrible news in general; perhaps even worse than initially thought.

I will be continuing to go through regular chemo, radiation, and potentially some other experimental drug treatments over the next weeks and months while getting recurring MRIs to check on the tumor's growth. The hope is that it can continue to be held off for as long as possible and doesn't become exponentially more malignant.

10

My body is working tirelessly to keep me alive, but I feel as though I am merely sitting here, doing nothing. I wake up. I check my phone. I take care of this and that. I watch TV. I eat. I read. I walk. I think. I write. I sometimes visit the doctor and get the same tests done, over and over. I rotate around on the wheel of my routine.

At times, I have found myself wondering if it's merely a waste to live anymore at all. I wonder if I'm just wasting days at this point. But in wondering this, I catch myself. I realize that I've always felt like that, long before my diagnosis. Even when my life was supposedly going well in the general sense, the same inescapable sense of a wasting time permeated me.

Throughout my life, I've found myself at different levels of success and in different daily routines; but all of which elicited the same or similar feelings. When I wasn't doing well, I felt like I wasn't doing enough. When I was doing well, I felt like I wasn't doing enough. When I was having fun, I felt guilty for not working. When I was working, I felt guilty for not having fun. The feeling of dissatisfaction and wasting time adapted to every aspect of my life. I wonder, then, what really constitutes wasting time? Does anyone really know a wasted day from a valuable one? In a world that lacks clear direction and as part of a species that is incapable of knowing what anything might truly mean or cause, isn't the value of time entirely relative on any given day in any given moment? At bottom, I'm the only person who has ever decided if I wasted a day or not.

If I enjoyed one of the days in the last couple weeks in which I did nothing other than read, was it wasted? Perhaps five months ago, prior to my diagnosis, it would have felt somewhat wasted. But now, it doesn't feel like it. Perhaps this is just my way of justifying or dignifying my circumstantial inertness, but I'd propose the opposite: that my enjoyed inertness is a way of justifying this suggestion.

If one enjoys or values the time they *wasted*, did they really waste it?

Of course, at a certain point when taken to an extreme, the answer could be yes. But more generally, a wasted day cannot be predicated on any objective accomplishment or activity alone. Rather, it is to be based on the experience or outcome of the day, essentially measured against one's expectations or interests of the day. An arbitrary quality. What we do with our time, then, is only as important as how we consider what we do with our time.

I wonder now how many days I wasted thinking I wasted days?

How many days I made bad for no reason other than thinking they were bad, overlooking how good I could have made them by simply recognizing how good they already were?

Personally, I don't see this as an excuse to lay around on the couch and do nothing. Nor do I see it as an argument against productivity. I see it as a *truth* that must be worked with on the individual level. If I feel like I wasted a day, then perhaps it is worth considering, if possible, how to either spend my days differently or look at my days differently. Each person is different here, though. And that's the important part. The value of one's time should not be predicated on anyone else's preference for how it should be spent, as if anyone truly knew.

Who knows what we are working towards—individually and collectively? The motivation to succeed is healthy and fine and perhaps worth indulging, but the reality is, underneath it, there is a force of life pushing us forward on some endless cycle that none of us understand and appears to go nowhere. If one's motivation is the endgame output of it all—some imagined conclusive, objective, final value—it will all be for nothing.

Ultimately, from the simply absurd to the complexly absurd, we fill our days with stuff merely to keep busy. An idle mind is the devil's workshop, so they say. Which is also to say that one's being, in its most basic, fundamental condition, is that of anguish. That to sit with one's self, alone with one's thoughts, is to experience the nausea of existing as one's self. It's as if instead of becoming nauseous from motion in life, we become nauseas from motionlessness. Thus, our default mode is misery, and everything is but an effort of distraction. Whether it's building a model train or running a Fortune 500 company, everything is merely a method of keeping one's self from one's self, staying in motion for motion's sake.

At a certain point, the reason for productivity and activity is merely to facilitate a sense of meaning and motion in life, which, in turn, facilitates the ability to say the day was not wasted. But it is only this that deems a day unwasted: the individual belief rather than the end-of-day output. And so it is of essential importance, in my opinion, that one recognizes this and synchronizes themselves with their particular value and preference of motion, but does so solely by themselves, for themselves.

We should work and strive for progress, not for anything else other than our own experience of progression and synchronicity with our self and our life's movement. We are wired to feel alive and vital in the thralls of progression and movement towards something that aligns with the strange barometer of meaning inside each of us. But there is no meaning beyond that. At least none that we have access to. The motivation for something—for anything—must then be found in what is immediately expressed and experienced in the present now. For some, this means a rapid, fast-paced, *large-scale* lifestyle; and for others, it means a slow-paced, simple, quiet lifestyle. Both are equally meaningless to the universe and both are equally meaningful to those who live well in it.

CHAPTER 3:
HONESTY & THE LACK THEREOF

11

It would seem as though the bulk of life is spent trying to avoid life. We hide our lives from each other. From ourselves. We avoid facing the bleakness and sadness. It's as if we are all covering our ears from the ringing inside our own head; or closing our eyes as we are getting punched in the face. It's a reasonable, natural reaction. But it doesn't help.

As a young child, I recall a deep, unexplainable sadness. I remember crying fairly often for no reason. When my mother asked me why I was crying, I remember saying I didn't know. Then I asked her why I was for no reason. I don't recall ever getting an answer, probably because there isn't one. At the time, I had no idea it was possible that my mother likely felt the same and didn't know why either. I didn't know that I was experiencing the default of life's modes: that cyclical rotation of anxiety and tedium inescapably linked with being. I thought there was something wrong with me and I was supposed to exist outside of this.

I would imagine that at the time, my mother at least had a hunch that this is what I was experiencing. But what mother, if they even realize it, tells her young child this? That life is not happiness or comfort, but the opposite. And so, she didn't. And I went on feeling sad and confused about why I was sad and confused.

Now, almost thirty years later, I feel the same. The same nausea never left. I now know the reason, though. The irony is, as a seven-year-old child, I was partly right about it being for no reason. In truth, the sadness and anxiety of existence has no reason. But that is its reason: that it has none. That it can hover over and in anything and everything and yet, refuses to properly justify itself. And because of this, we experience it. If it had a reason, it wouldn't be so sad or miserable. Sadness, anxiety, and misery with an explanation is easy. Easy to track, source, justify, and potentially overcome. Sadness and anxiety with no clear reason is impossible. It's like fighting air. And so, the absurd reasonless-ness of it becomes the worst possible reason.

What's worse about this fact is that it takes most of us a while to ever properly realize and come to terms with it, if at all. I lived many early years of my life suffering for no good reason, thinking that there must be a good reason, and consequently, making it way worse. I thought I could fight air and win. But I was only hopelessly tiring myself out and feeling like a fool.

12

I would argue that no person with a functioning human brain lives without deeply and frequently pondering the absurdity of their existence. And yet, to talk about life directly, intensely, or honestly in this way is somehow almost always out of place. For some reason, everyone has this hunch that everyone is fucked, and yet, very few of us can even say so. Perhaps if more of us did, less of us would feel as though we were. Perhaps we would spend more time trying to learn how to live with our condition rather than always trying to escape it. The communication of such honest topics is left mostly to non-commercial artists, drunken conversations, therapy sessions, writers, philosophers, and the crazy people on the streets.

The reason for this is not that we don't all know what the human condition feels like, but that the human condition overwhelms us so heavily that we often flee from it at all costs. We often bury it beneath the chatter of new careers, promotions, pop culture updates, cars, sports games, gossip, weather, properly-cooked chicken, and all the rest.

13

I think everyone is, at bottom, *philosopher* first. The artist, writer, priest, atheist, businessman, athlete, cashier, homeless person—everyone is a *philosopher* first. Which is to say that every decision is a philosophical one. Every perception and belief one has and how they came to have them. Even believing one is not a philosopher is an act of philosophy. All acts are philosophical.

Of course, in the more formal sense of the term, not everyone is. Not everyone is studying or producing works pertaining to technical philosophical terms or ideas related to metaphysics, existence, etc. However, I believe the only difference between the philosophers that are in books or on panels and the philosopher in everyone's head is the same difference between the singers on the radio and the singer in every car singing along. It's not as if everyone doesn't feel the same yearning to sing, but some people are just better at understanding the music theory and making it sound good. And those same people dedicate their lives to continually understanding more and making it sound even better. Whereas most of those who do not, keep it in the car. As they likely should.

To be good at using language, logic, perception, analysis, and self-understanding in the form of creating and sharing ideas is a talent; an intellectual aptitude, perhaps. But it's not a separation. The source of motivation out of which high-level philosophical discourse emerges is in us all. The same motivation that compels us to sing along with our favorite songs that we can't quite sing right. I think, if anything, this world needs the humanities and sciences to be viewed in a similar light as music. A world in which adolescences are encouraged to engage in an eclectic mix of concepts and ideas so it's easier and more normal to at least want to listen and try to sing along.

I know this might have helped me.

14

At thirty-five, I'm not sure I can say that I've ever had a completely honest conversation with anyone, including myself. I've lived in fear and limitation, always catering to the circumstances of my biology, emotional states, desires, surrounding people, social systems, environments, and realms of being unknown. Somewhere within this flurry exists some core *thing* that yearns to be understood. Maybe not understood so much as honestly seen, observed, or interacted with. Even writing this right now is an example of just that. The yearning to try; to try to express the present version of myself to the world with an effort of complete honesty. At least as much honesty as I have access to. However, like most people, I struggle to do so; to find the parts of myself that are buried deep. The parts that I pretend aren't part of "I" when I utter the letter. The parts that I hate, fear, or don't know. It is these aspects of the *self*, however, that yearn for the daytime light. And although we might never be fully understood by anyone, I think it is one of our few worthy endeavors and duties to try to discover and bare as much of our true self as we can; to unendingly dig towards the core of oneself and the cores of others; confronting, exploring, and expressing it, however hard or dark it may be. Not because there's some ultimate resolution in the task, but because it helps provide the ability to confront the likeliness that there isn't.

Nearly every other task outside of honest conversation, writing, philosophy, art, self-expression and the like—every other activity and every other venture—is often an attempt to run from, not towards one's life and one's self. I, like all people, have a longing to run from myself. But it's obvious after a certain point that there is no escape.

15

We don't share what's hard. We don't admit what's weak or vulnerable or horrible about being who we are. We rarely mean what we say. We answer, "How are you doing?" with, "Good," when we aren't anywhere close. And so on.

This all makes sense in commonplace conversation. In most cases, we seem to just burden others with our sorrows and complexities. And so, we often can't be honest without also being insensitive or selfish, and yet, at the same time, in many cases we need to be honest with others so that they can be honest with us and relieve some of their own sorrows and complexities. It's a gear system that needs everyone involved for it to turn at all, but rarely does anyone even try to start it because rarely does it feel opportune.

We seem to be stuck in this conflict between needing everyone to say how they really feel—that they're not okay—and no one wanting to deal with such a fact. We've all agreed to play this game. To hide our trash in our room. To an extent, this is fair. But when all the world's trash is hidden, and each of us are secretly sleeping in our own stench every night, it's easy to feel like we're the only one that smells and everyone else doesn't. Like we are weird and broken and inferior to the rest of the world. Of course, however, we are mostly all the same in this. We are all the same in our uncertainty of whether or not we are different than everyone else.

In truth, there is a little soft, sensitive core in every one of our chests that needs the attention, sympathy, love, and honesty of others. A core that rarely receives anything at all. And as a result, we all often feel like we are lost and strange and abandoned. One can only question how we all feel like this if we all feel like this.

Sometimes we need to listen to happy music to feel good. And sometimes we need to listen to sad music to feel good. Sometimes we need clichés of motivation and positivity. And sometimes we need to face the bleaker realities to understand what we might actually be.

We can't always be consciously at battle with the darker components of our self, nor can we always burden others with them. However, we also can't always hide from them and pretend they're not there.

Generally, this is what art and literature and philosophy are for. Every good book I've read. Every good movie I've watched. Every good piece of comedy. Every beautiful art piece. All threw me into the conversations I needed to have but could never have with anyone directly. They revealed to me that the conversations I often had with myself weren't so exclusively with myself, but rather, with some strange collective substrate that builds and binds each one of us. How great and divine these experiences were and how badly I could have used more. How badly the world could use more.

It is not necessarily truth that this world needs more of, but perhaps an infinite amount more honesty. A world where the conversations had through literature and art are more commonly had in other mainstream medias and life in general. Perhaps a world where honest expression is more focal. More central. Less avoided by friends and families. Less pervaded by cheap, cash grab Hollywood projects. Less watered down and commodified by businesses that relentlessly pander to market themselves into *scale*.

Could such a world exist? Who knows?

16

Over the last several weeks, some family and friends that I don't normally see have visited. I sort of wish they hadn't. It's a nice gesture and one might naturally think that company is to be desired during such a difficult time, but I mostly feel weird and bad for disrupting their lives, and most of the time, I'd rather be alone.

It's funny: every time people I don't normally see visit me, it reminds me that I'm dying. The funny part is that despite this reminder, everyone asks me how I'm doing, and I say, "Good." Like strangers checking out at a grocery store.

17

Earlier today, I was with my little cousin Henry. He's only two years younger than me, and it's weird calling an adult man who is bigger than you "little," but technically he's my little cousin. I don't normally see my cousins or aunts and uncles, including Henry, all that often. Maybe once or twice a year for Christmas and other one-off occasions. I've never really been that close with any of my family outside of my parents and grandparents. In total, I have fourteen cousins and eight aunts and uncles. I don't really know or particularly feel that comfortable with any of them.

The concept of family is strange, really; to have a lifelong relationship with people you don't really know and have nothing in common with other than arbitrary bloodlines. It's like friends of friends, but you didn't even choose the first friends. I know it's not like that for everyone. But it's like that for me. In any case, Henry is the only cousin I've ever been in some way close to. When we were about six to twelve years old, we would hang out together, but grew apart not long after that. Ever since, we have had the sort of relationship where it seems like we're on the same page but can't really tell. A common relationship amongst people, I suppose. As a result, though, talking with him has always been kind of an effort. In nearly all interactions with him, and with mostly anyone in general for that matter, I would always think rather heavily about everything I said, trying at great lengths to ensure that I said the right things. I would always know that there's no real reason for this; to be so eccentrically careful about my words. Nor would I ever have any reason to play a character and impress him or anyone else with some methodical version of myself. But regardless, every time I saw Henry, and anyone like him, I always became anxious about what I said and how I came off. It was inescapable. I could tell myself beforehand that there was nothing to be anxious about. No reason to care. And yet, when I was in it, I'd be anxious and careful as if such a state had no regard for rational orders and control.

Prior to today, I hadn't seen Henry since last Christmas. Today, him and his sister (my other cousin) and his parents (my aunt and uncle) came to visit.

At some point in their visit, everyone else left to go pick up some food and it was just Henry and me. We sat for a little and talked about the show that we were watching on TV. The conversation was simple, but funny enough, it was one of the best conversations I've had in a long time. Certainly, the best I've had with him. We talked about what made the show stupid but interesting. We talked about how life was funny like that. We talked about personal experiences we both had that mirrored the show. We just talked. I didn't think much about anything at all other than what I wanted to say. And it seemed as if he was doing the same. More or less uninhibited, but respectful. It was nice.

It's strange talking to people. It's hard, but mostly just because we try so hard to be good at it. I would suppose that the conversation with Henry was better because I simply didn't care all that much about how good it was. I mean, I talk to myself all the time and, although it's exhausting, it certainly isn't hard in the same way. And I think some of the best conversations I've ever had are one's I've had with myself. It seems like the more we try to predict and control how we are perceived or understood, the worse off we are. In an effort to say the right things, we often avoid saying the real things. Which are usually the right things. You become a photo of a photo of a photo of yourself. A low-res, synthetic version, void of whatever uniqueness that makes you worthwhile and interesting and capable of enriched connection.

I am not entirely sure why it takes dying to feel like you don't have try so hard to say what you think; to talk like yourself. We seem to always wait until it's too late to properly realize it's too late.

I'm not suggesting one should always say what they think, because a lot of the times what we think isn't even what we mean or want or agree with. And furthermore, there are consequences to going around saying what you want all the time that should be considered. Like everything, there's a balance. And like most balances, it's damn near impossible to know and sustain. But it does, however, seem to often be skewed towards the side of self-restriction as opposed to openness. And I would argue that, at a certain point, if it should be skewed towards any side, one is much better off being themselves and being disliked, than not and being liked.

Trying to be liked is a zero-sum game. If you say things because you think it's what people want to hear and you're wrong, then they don't like you. And if you say things because you think it's what people want to hear and you're right, then they like a version of you that isn't real. Both are losses. At least in the case where you say what you want to say, you're either liked or disliked for who you really are in that moment.

I wonder if my cousin and I lost closeness with each other because of this. Because of my lack of honesty and ability to be myself. I wonder if I lost closeness with a lot of people because of this. Because I tried too hard to be someone that wasn't real. At a certain point, you can't be close with someone who doesn't really exist.

It's sort of pathetic that we care so much about what others think that we are willing to sacrifice who we really are. And yet, at the same time, it's sort of beautiful. It's a paradoxical testament to our simultaneous weakness and strength: wanting to be liked.

Ultimately, I think being liked in the full complete sense that we desire is impossible anyway. In the same way you'll never fully like yourself because you know who you really are, you'll never like anyone else that you know completely; likewise, no one else will ever like you completely; because everyone is some amount unlikable.

18

The relationship between our self, our perception of our self, and our perception of other people and things interacting with our self forms the constantly changing self that we are. A self that we can never quite grasp because it is always in the thralls of this feedback loop.

We don't create who we are. And we can't hold onto who we are. But we must own and express it in every moment.

CHAPTER 4:
THE ART OF LIVING WITH YOURSELF

19

Over the past months, I have spent a good amount of time with friends and family. Close and extended. It's been nice, but I have had a weird, increasing desire to be alone.

The desire itself isn't weird per se because I've had it most of my life. At least on some level. Generally, I like people. But most of the time, from a distance. I enjoy my occasional doses of company and socializing, but I've always preferred my time skewed much more towards solitude, even when I've been in relationships, which of course has caused its fair share of problems.

What's weird isn't the desire, but that, if anything, it's increased. For some reason, I would have imagined that it would have decreased with the foresight of my early death. That with only a little bit of time left—with the fact that I'll never be with anyone else ever again and never have the chance to say another word to anyone else's ear—I would want to spend as much time with other people as possible. But I mostly just want to be with myself.

Maybe that isn't strange. If during my life I wanted solitude, why wouldn't I during my death?

In truth, I don't feel that anyone else could come into the room I'm writing in right now and do or say anything that could help.

Being by yourself a lot is typically branded as lonely, but I don't feel lonely. Never have, really. Of course, being alone and feeling alone are two very different things. You don't necessarily feel alone just because you are literally. And you don't necessarily feel close to others just because you are around them. The difference, obviously, isn't physical proximity, but the depth of one's capacity to connect with the *thing* we are all a part of. A generally isolated person who derives this sense best when they're alone is better off than a person who is always in a big group but, without knowing it, would enjoy their time more being alone.

Admittedly, I would imagine everyone is somewhat different in their social calibrations and preferences, but for me, there has always been a desire for some amount of quiet and peace and the control that would allow for both. This is never fully possible, but you really only get anywhere close when you're alone. When you finally get to hear and play with your thoughts, undisturbed. In all times of my life, especially now, I have needed this; for the noise of the world to be quiet enough so to properly hear the noise that persists inside my own head. The static buzz that hums in the background of everything that you can only really notice when nearly everything else turns down. When you sit with this isolated noise of self long enough, you eventually learn how to better live with it; to notice it enough to become more used to it; to finally deal with the thoughts that have been pleading for your attention; to discover how to properly be yourself and make use of it.

Mostly everyone is afraid of living and dying alone, but it seems that few people are afraid of living and dying without ever really knowing the person they're afraid of being alone with. At a certain point, if one wants to be okay with themselves, one's closest friend must be solitude.

I don't detest friendship, although I do find it somewhat over-rated. For me, there is no denying the immeasurable value that good, true friendship and company has had in my life. I don't know many people who would argue against the value of good friend-ship—even the most isolated people in the world. A person needs at least one to a few people to be there for them, and for them to be there for. Or at least the sense that they are. But good friendship and solitude are not antonymous. Good friendship forms out of those who know themselves well enough to create and maintain good friendship. The person who has yet to find any comfort in themselves will gnaw and pull at others in hopes of finding it, forming a sort of addictive dependency on their relationships in which they put the weight of their own wellbeing on the shoulders of others, which no good friendship can come from.

I desire the good company of others, but certainly not more than I desire the good company of myself. And some level of deep solitude in life is likely required to properly make good company of yourself. And ironically, then, some level of solitude is perhaps also required to make good company of anyone else.

One good friend is worth a hundred friends. Comfort with solitude is worth thousands.

At the end of the day, we're always isolated in ourselves in our own isolated sections of the universe. We are all empirically alone inside our heads, from birth till death. Even in a crowd of thousands of people, every person is ultimately a solitary receiver of everything. Everything and everyone is experienced individually, skull by skull, moment by moment, once, for all eternity. And so, you are your only real hope.

20

You can be the best you can be, but you can never be better than you are. And you only know how good you are by finding out how good you aren't. It's nice to say, "You can do it." It's a leading staple of modern platitudes. But some of us can't do *it*. And some of us can, but never find out what it is that we can.

The truth is, no one knows what anyone can or can't do until they have or haven't done it. Some people choose to do the wrong things their whole life, wasting it away pursuing something that they were never meant to do. Some people give up or die just moments before finding out that they were right all along. And some people just might not be equipped to do anything particularly *great*. But the point isn't that you shouldn't try. The point is that if you have any interest and any ability to, you should. Because it's the only way you'll ever know. And as Charles Bukowski said, "If you're going to try, go all the way. Otherwise, don't even start." Worst cases are, you're either unsuccessful because you never tried, or you're unsuccessful because you tried and were wrong. But only the latter contains any chance at all. And it is perhaps the only chance worth fighting for.

You will doubt yourself every step of the way, including after you achieve the thing, if you do. You will remain confused, anxious, unsure, unhappy, and mortal. But you will have taken this life and justified it. You will have done the only thing that appears worth doing. You will have taken it and made it something you deem interesting or meaningful or helpful or worthwhile. You will have transmuted the material of the universe from nothing to something; an act that is exclusive to the consciousness *something* inside your head.

21

The entire universe came from apparent nothingness, coming into existence for either some reason or no reason, both equally arbitrary.

This particular galaxy came about through some unknown, random order and mix of matter, gas clouds, dust, and gravity; collapsing, clumping, consuming, and growing. This planet through another random, unknown sub-sequence of disturbed gas and dust particles all sent into a swirling disk of potential, forging the sun and stars, molting balls of gas and liquid, cooling and solidifying, all with just the right mix of stuff in the right position of space to eventually form and later be delivered with water and ice by wet comets. This was all done with no more or less chance than throwing a bag of sand into the wind and planning where each grain goes.

The amount of randomness at play in every moment of the universe is the same amount of randomness at play inside the skulls of each and every person. And through this randomness—this chaos—the self is born.

One could imagine they were born 3,000.2 miles west from where they were actually born, to the parents closest to that point, and into the body and mind of one of those parent's children. You would be the person that that child has and continues to turn into. That completely different person, however good or bad, talented or untalented, successful or unsuccessful, miserable or less miserable. You could hate that person. But through the same strange, inexplicable, arbitrary odds of cosmic circumstance, you could have just as easily been them instead of you.

Everyone is who they are by complete chance. You did not choose anything that started the sequence of who you are and will become. No one did.

However, it is possible that we do possess the choice to live in accordance with the person we are, however we came to be it. And perhaps that's all that really matters.

22

It appears reasonable to argue that perhaps there are variations in the resources and conditions of each individual, and thus, one's ability to trust and/or express themselves is not always equal. If a person becomes who they are through a *random*, natural function beyond their will, it is also possible that one's own ability to understand, defend, or tap into who they are is a part of a *random*, natural function beyond one's will.

However, even if we don't have control over the circumstances of who we are—even if we don't have control over how capable we are in truly knowing who we are—perhaps so long as one authentically and honestly stands in their own position of confusion and limitation, they still remain in accordance with their true self. In which case, despite any lack of choice or will or understanding in becoming who we are, it is through the self-honest attempt to confront and express such lack of choice and will and understanding that matters to the honest expression of one's self.

Self-expression isn't about choosing, controlling, or knowing yourself. It's about trying to be honest about how much you believe you do or don't. It's about being yourself in all its confusions.

No one else will ever have the same mix of stuff I have and no one else will ever experience this reality from the other side of my skull, for all eternity. This goes for every human being and every living thing to ever traverse this material reality.

If a group of people looked out of the same telescope, fixed in the same position, and pointing at the same sky, no one would ever see the same sky. Given that only one person can look out at a time, everyone would see the same sky at different times, and thus, see a sky comprised of different molecules in different positions. Of course, phenomenally, it would appear to be the same sky, but in actuality, it would be a different sky. More importantly, though, each person would be filtering their perception of the sky through their own unique assemblage of present and prior mental states. Their particular mood at the time of looking. Their particular understandings and frameworks for what a sky is and means. Their particular mode of thinking and accumulation of residual influences. And anything else. All mixed together.

Of course, every moment of everything works this same way. Not one person has or will ever experience the same as what anyone else has or will ever experience. Even if it's the same exact thing at the same exact time.

I own nothing that is completely mine except the way I experience everything. Each one of us owns that one thing, and that one thing alone. A particular order of particular experiences. And perhaps it is more like it owns us, seeing as how we didn't choose any of it.

Ultimately, each of us has a one-off ticket to the show. A show that we get to experience from our exclusively designated seat in the theater. And so, we must enjoy and share what we see as best we can. For our sake. For everyone else in the crowd's sake. For the show's sake.

To live having never expressed and tried to do what one uniquely wants to do with their experience—what one interprets and believes in, what one sees and feels—would be to live a life as an unclaimed self. A life unfulfilled. A nominal improvement from never having lived at all.

Life is chaotic, destructive, disappointing, uncontrollable, and often barely tolerable. And so, it is arguably one of our few great, important tasks to not make it any more so. To not be enamored by hallow desires and false promises. To not be encumbered by unnecessary chaos and misery that we have no stake or sense of meaning in. To not detach ourselves from the faint embers of youthful interests. At a certain point, this is the only good fight worth fighting.

This is not to reduce the intense, sometimes horrible, complexity and difficulty of successfully doing so. But it is to say: what else could possibly be the point to any of this torture? Every sore neck, spiral of anxiety, spell of depression, broken heart, loss of a loved one, endurance of self; what justification could any of it have if not the pursuance of one's own truth and meaning and interests?

The thing we are motivated by, then, must not be wealth nor status nor fame nor happiness nor much of anything other than the realization of ourselves and our personal interests and meaning. Whatever that might mean and wherever it might have come from. The outward reflection of our most honest, candid sense of *truth* and meaning appears, to me, to be all there is.

Why we need to exhibit this external representation of self— why we need meaning, why we need anything at all—is unclear. But the desire to create appears fundamental in us all. To render a reflection of the internal into the external in a feedback loop of self-perception and understanding. If there is any real source of solace and self-knowledge, it is to be found in the that; art in its broadest sense. All the forms it takes—painting, music, literature, film, and all the rest.

Of course, in the act of creating, expressing, and living as one's true self, one risks something we all dread: rejection. And worse yet, rejection on the deepest and most personal level. But if the fear of being rejected keeps us from our self, are we not, in essence, rejecting our self first? The only person we truly and inescapably have to live with. And in this, we risk living without ever fully exploring our self. Never fully being our self. Dying as someone who never saw the world and who the world never got a chance to see.

What the creative process does is paradoxically show us how strong and beautiful we are by showing us how we can face and share how pathetic and weak we are.

Ultimately, if someone has been alive for any amount of time, their take on this world is valid and worthwhile. One can be ashamed of it. One can feel like they are foolish or wrong. One can feel like an imposter. But they should share themselves anyway. In any way they see fit. Because everyone is some level foolish and wrong, everyone is some level ashamed, and everyone is some level imposter. Even all the *greats* throughout history. The line between the *greats* and the *ordinaries* is far thinner than most of us assume. And if anyone has the right to embrace and share themselves, everyone does.

The world needs our best attempts at our true self. We need our best attempts. To live deeply and honestly. To feel and express that very substrate that builds and binds us. To attempt to do something that is at least slightly different from anything anyone else has ever done. To say something that no one else has ever quite said. To forge through the darkness with a light of one's own design. To mine into the senses and the nature of one's self, face the confusions and horrors, and then bare it to the world unyieldingly. For me, that is what it means to realize the self. It's not an answer. It's not a state. It's not a happiness or even a success. It's a continuous process. A fusion of chaos and equanimity.

23

I think one of the few, true, beautiful solaces in life is music. I don't imagine I'm unique in such a claim. But I would probably go so far to say that if music was all the good there was in this life, it would be enough.

A lot of things touch the soul. A lot of different forms of art, images of beauty, thoughts and conversations of intellect, moments of love and lust; but none are quite as consistent and reliable as music. Music is perhaps the easiest and the least likely to miss or let me down.

Kurt Vonnegut once wrote, "If I should die, God forbid, let this be my epitaph: The only proof he needed for the existence of God was music." I don't think music is proof of God any more or less than death and torture is proof of none, and I would bet that Vonnegut meant this sentiment somewhat facetiously. But I do think it's proof of something. And I think that's what Vonnegut meant anyway.

Music is proof that there is something; some divine capacity of humanity; some frequency of sound that exists hidden in the nothingness of space, discovered, created, and/or transmitted by humans that brings us all to an indescribable sensation of understanding or love or solace or vitality.

Each human is a receiver and transmitter of this connection. And music is proof of that; the god and disciple that is every individual human being.

24

In truth, from enough distance, none of us matter. But by the same token, from a close enough distance, we are all that matters. Everything and everyone eventually dissolves into the ether of insubstantiality. Everyone, at their time, will be forgotten. Some in a couple decades after they're gone. Some in a millennium. Some before any memories of them even had a chance to form.

In the bigger picture, it does not matter how important anyone is now, has been, or will be. At some point, there will be no one to decide or remember what important even is. But this means that along with all our successes and moments of beauty, each of our failures and moments of horridness will be forgotten as well. All of what feels like the end of the *world* will ultimately confront the end of the world itself. This is sad, of course. However, in it exists a certain freedom to put everything on the table right now. Not for some imagined notion of some future, but rather, for the very real sliver of right now that we actually have. The only thing we have any reason to believe in: our self and our one-off juncture of all of time and space.

25

After a certain point, most accomplishments are only as good as the stress that went into them. When you feel the misery of the inevitable moments of tribulation towards a larger objective, you're experiencing the buildup of the value of the thing. This is perhaps a complicated way of saying the cliché, "Nothing good comes easy." But it's perhaps worth complicating. It's not simply to say that nothing good comes easy, but that often things only become good because they aren't easy. And perhaps good things aren't even really that good. It could be argued that if the value of accomplishing a thing is predicated, to at least some extent, on how difficult the effort is in accomplishing it, then the value is found in the effort, not the thing. In other words, the hard, challenging, and often miserable parts of accomplishing something good IS the good thing. And the accomplishment is just the embodiment of it. Another perhaps complicated way of rephrasing the cliché, "It's the journey, not the destination that matters." But again, perhaps worth complicating. It's not that the destination doesn't matter or matters less than the journey, but that without the journey, it doesn't even exist. Which is all to say that, although it's perhaps a natural response to want to avoid the responsibility and stress and difficult parts of things, to do so is to wish away the whole point.

To make life *good* is not to make it so that stress and misery no longer exist, but to make it so that they exist for something one has some level of belief, interest, or stake of meaning in. To transmute the inescapable, inevitable suffering and hardship of life into something that has a fighting chance of making it worthwhile.

26

Those who speak of what they are doing with boastful confidence are likely either deeply consumed by their insecurities or deeply consumed by their self-esteem. Or both. In most cases (not all), what they speak of and what they claim is rarely real. And what is real is rarely held together well enough to withstand the true test of reality.

People who need to boastfully claim their future successes before they have them will likely never obtain such successes, and if they do, they will likely never keep them. And people who continue to boast or posture heavily on their successes while they have them—their loudness is only a sign that they still have not found anything in any of it. They need to acquire the attention and admiration of others to compensate for the little amount they have been able to acquire of themselves.

Inevitably, at least some amount of arrogance or self-importance is a side effect of successes. Personally, I have exhibited my fair share of posturing and hubris, at least in some form or another. It's not easy to maintain a proper awareness and reign over it. And *proud* confidence is not always bad a thing either. But to predicate your successes and character and social standing on such, only increases the farcical load-to-bear on the house of cards that you almost certainly exist inside.

There's a fine line between acting confidently and being confident. And the relationship isn't always clear. I agree with the value of being confident and talking confidently, but how confident one acts and appears is, of course, not necessarily proportional to how confident one truly is. Often it's inversely proportional. And oftentimes, you can't tell the difference.

It is, in my opinion, of great importance to know this and tentatively trust, follow, and agree with anyone on the merit of their convictional attitude and articulation. And it is perhaps of equal importance to keep a steadfast eye on your own. Actions and results are the only real forms of proof, if any, for one's true ability and character. Everyone knows this, and yet, we seem to so often succumb to the spell of others' convictions, as well as the spell of our own desire to act on conviction we don't have.

27

Between the medications, the strange daily schedules, the anxiety, and the lack of much future responsibility, it's been harder and harder to wake up recently. Or maybe it's been harder to fall asleep. Maybe both. Either way, I've been waking up later. Normally around twelve or so. And then I just lay in bed for a while, not getting up until around one. That's obviously late, but when you go to bed around four or later, what are you supposed to do? It's still only seven or eight hours of sleep. The only thing I'm really losing is daylight, not hours.

I still feel sort of guilty, though.

I've always been a night person and a late riser. And my profession has allowed me the luxury to live this way. To schedule my days and nights how I please. I think it's in the nature of writers and artists in general to perhaps prefer evenings to work. But whether it's early or late, the goal is always just to find some time when most of the world is turned off and all distractions have been minimized to the point at which you almost feel like you shouldn't be awake, which weirdly creates some sort of motivation to get stuff done, almost giving you the proud feeling that you're snatching the proverbial *early bird worm*. The phrase is, "The early bird gets the worm," but it's just the same for the bird that still hasn't gone to sleep yet. It's really just about whoever's up when mostly no one else is.

For me, it's always been late at night. And I've always found my fair share of worms.

Why does it seem that the majority of the world argues so heavily for getting up early? And why is it that those that do, seem to so often boast about it? Mostly no one ever brags about staying up till five, but seemingly a good percentage of people who get up at five, claim it as a personality trait, despite it potentially meaning the same thing.

If one's argument is that waking up early equates to a more *successful* day, then that would have to mean that waking up earlier equated to more hours in the day. Which it doesn't. If I went to bed at four and got up at eleven, while someone else went to bed at ten and got up at five, we would have both slept and been awake the same number of hours.

And even if we weren't awake the same number of hours, for the claim to still hold any validity, more waking hours would have to equate to a more productive day. Which it doesn't. How well hours are used is what matters here. And working a well-focused and well-executed three hours can almost certainly outperform the average person's nine.

And finally, a more productive day doesn't equate to a better or more valuable day. Life is obviously not merely a game of output. What exactly it is a game of is unclear. But it is certainly not any one thing.

Despite all of this essentially being nonsense, and knowing that it is, I still often feel a pressure to get up earlier, which is perhaps a testament to how easily we feel the need to collect in the same drains of life. The same routines. The same cycles. The same orders. I get it. It makes sense. But it's tiresome. It's a deprivation of any chance at potentially greater slivers of daily routines and lives.

I would probably concede to the fact that many people who wake up at eleven in the morning are typically unproductive, unreliable, or unemployed. But an equal amount, if not more, are artists, comedians, night managers, writers, security guards, dying, and so on. I express disdain towards those that say one must get up early, but I am not arguing for a lazy life. I am arguing for one's own life. It isn't even about the time one goes to bed or the time one gets up. It's about the principle. The seemingly constant pressure to mold one's life according to the standard norms. Of course, there are obvious reasons for standard norms of time and routines and so on. Namely, so that everyone that needs to be on the same schedule is on the same schedule. But not everyone needs to be. And for those that do not, it should not matter.

I say know your own terms and wake and sleep on them; live and die on them. If you're wrong, you'll live for yourself and likely be no worse off than just about everyone else. If you're right, you'll live for yourself and possibly be phenomenally better than everyone else.

How absurd it is that people impose their own ways of living onto others as if they knew any better? Sure, it's fantastic to make and consider recommendations, but no one can nor should impose any way with certainty. If anything, doing so only suggests a displeasure with how one lives; a misery that they feel tricked or confined by. And subsequently, they feel that no one else should live or try any other way and be any better off.

For some reason, it often appears that the result of much of our own unhappiness is to make or want others equally unhappy, as if other people's unhappiness could ever really make our own any less.

Staying clear of this both as the predator and the prey is perhaps a worthy endeavor. Of course, who am I to say?

CHAPTER 5:
EVERYTHING IS A MYSTERY NOTHING CAN SOLVE
Religion, Science, & the Plight of Humankind

28

Recent MRIs have revealed nothing but more bad news. The tumor has grown back and seems to be growing rather aggressively. It's mutated or evolved or whatever into what they've now diagnosed as a stage 4 glioblastoma. The worst kind of brain tumor. It hasn't responded well to many of the treatments. Any specks of remaining hope for this thing to not go worst-case have almost entirely been cleared off the table. The odds of me living past five years are basically gone. The odds of me living past one are up in the air.

I'm going to a new doctor at a new hospital in about a week. There is supposed to be some sort of uniquely different radiation treatment that might be more effective towards further mitigation. Supposedly this particular treatment can be surprisingly effective for cases like mine and could potentially, hopefully, keep me alive a little longer. We'll have to see.

29

At some point for most people, a realization occurs. A realization that the answers you have access to—the answers you're given—ultimately, are all nonsense. Not only incomplete, but mostly not even answers at all. Everyone who has taught you what you know, fundamentally knows nothing about anything. To truly know what anything is, one must first know what a *thing* is. And no one really does.

We are all walking around completely clueless, screaming or laughing inside our heads at any given moment. We are all just looking at the skin of existence through a magnifying glass, unable to step back and see the whole thing, and unable to open it up and see inside. We see but the surface, if even that, and yet we often talk and act as if we know exactly what it is.

At some point, the value of intelligence is no longer found in how much one knows, but how well one deals with how little they do. How one accepts how likely it is that their strongest held beliefs and sensibilities are just as likely to be as wrong and contrived as everything they disagree with and know to be nonsense.

30

Everyone needs advice, but not the kind of advice that anyone else can give them. Not even the kind that anyone can give themselves. Rather, the kind of advice that no one has access to. The advice that the world keeps from everyone; how to live and die.

31

Ever since my diagnosis, especially since it's become more obvious how things will go, everyone has been giving me their prescriptions for how to deal with and think about it all. It's mostly annoying, frankly. Being told things like, "It's natural to feel angry," or, "It's going to be okay," when you're not sure what's natural to feel and know for a fact it won't be okay, somehow all have the exact opposite effect of the intention. Mostly everyone is just trying to create their own reasons and justifications and sense of involvement. Trying to suppose their own understandings and explanations for the cruel, *reasonless* absurdity of my situation. I have heard it all. I have heard that I will be brought back as this or that. That a place in heaven awaits me. That it's my destiny and that there's a bigger picture for me in the universe. That everything has a reason. That God is calling me. That God has a plan. And all the rest. I let everyone share their peace, but I don't agree with much of any of it. I know it's mostly all for them anyway.

Everyone wants a reason and sense of comfort most when there is clearly no basis for any. The worst, honestly, are those who preach God to me in such an obvious time of godlessness. At least in terms of the God they're referring. It's one thing to preach hope but another to claim that the hope is found in some personified god-like figure; the same figure who would also have to be responsible for my early death. How could that make any sense, and how could that possibly make me feel any better?

If such a God existed, it wouldn't be consoling for me to care, believe, or know of him.

The only god I have ever had any proof of is me; and perhaps every other human I've encountered. Certainly, I do not believe myself or any other human to be God, but that is only because I do not believe in any god in that sense at all. In that sense, it seems far more obviously likely to me that we created God and not the other way around. What is more God-like than to create the notion of God itself?

Even if one were to say God placed the notion of God inside our heads, why our heads alone and not all the other living things that will never know of him? And furthermore, why did God also place the notion of no God or a different God inside our heads? To choose to follow him? If that choice were proof of God, then so would the lack of choice in a dog be the proof of none.

Would God exist if humans didn't? If there were only plants and *unconscious* animals; no one to call God God; no one to decide it must be a white, bearded man or four-armed Indian man or any of the rest; would any such gods exist at all? Unclear and impossible to know. But that's the point.

If there's any house of God, it is not the churches but the skulls of every person who can conceive of him.

In truth, who knows what God is beyond this? Beyond the mere exemplification of human's ability to consider and conceive of something beyond themselves. To try and squish the impossible size and shape of the universe inside their absurdly tiny, little brains.

As I approach the end of my life, I find myself wondering why we feel the need to worship or believe anything ultimate at all. To search for or cling to something certain when inevitably everything will be changed, lost, or misunderstood. To believe or worship wholly in something is not proof of anything other than the need to believe or worship. And it is perhaps my only belief that there appears to be no thing, object, or idea worthy of firm belief. Not even this one.

There is no belief, school of thought, idea, lifestyle, or *thing* that seems to hold up against the unending flux of this unattainable reality. Every belief and idea is but a rock extruding from a flowing river, destined to be eroded in time. Like new rocks appear and disappear, human meaning and belief are constantly lost, re-discovered, and re-created overtime.

I remember when I realized Santa Claus was not real. I wondered how my parents could hold such a lie over my head for so long. And moreover, how the entire world could. Pretty convincingly no less. Somehow everyone agreed to uphold this deceit towards me and all other children out of some moral determination that it was for the better good. But does anyone really know if it is for the better good? In telling me to believe in Santa, the world essentially told me that I was stupid and better off being so. But was I? I'll never know.

Of course, if I had known Santa was not real, I would not have believed in him. One is only as smart or as stupid as the information they have. Once I realized I had no proof of Santa and, furthermore, good reason to believe he wasn't real, I stopped believing in him. At that point, whether or not Santa was fun to believe in made no difference. You believe in something because you have good reason to. And you can't know what you don't know, and you can't unknow what you know once you do. And I know now that I know damn near nothing about anything. Just like everyone else.

For God and anything like it, one might say you don't need a reason to believe. You just need faith. But I say that's a reason. Faith is a reason. It's a reason for needing reasons unknown. And if the reason is nothing beyond needing a reason, then there is no good reason, and faith is nothing but a regressive loop that disintegrates into absurdity.

To believe in something you don't and can't know simply to make yourself feel better is a sign of hopelessness, not hope or good faith.

How many adults still believe in a Santa to sustain the same childish deceit to artificially inject fake hope and magic into life? As if living weren't hope enough and life didn't have enough real magic already. Doesn't the lack of certainty and understanding of *what* and *why* create enough magic on its own? Doesn't the mystery of everything create more magic than any contrived certainty? There is a night sky filled with glowing orbs of hot gas. A planet filled with water and green oxygenating apparatuses. A conscious entity behind every pair of human eyes. A universe of stuff and phenomena that could likely create an infinite list of wonders. All of which appeared out of apparent nothingness. There is an unending realm of questions and answers about what all this is and could be. And yet, many of us look towards contrived definitive concepts of reality to find wonder.

No truly rational person believes in ultimate certainty, meaning, or divinity of any specific form. How could they? What proof do they have that everyone else doesn't beyond the complacency of their own ego and need to placate their fear of truth or lack thereof?

It was out of the unknown that every god was made. And it is out of this same unknown that many, many more will be made and killed. But it is the unknown that is the magic. Not any specific god or idea that comes from it.

If we want to find anything sacred, it is the experience of our self right now in the midst of whatever perceptive state of this unknown we exist. The *now*. And it is not merely *this now* that we must revere, but the *whole now*. The flux of everything perceived through different windows of time and space.

One must revere and believe in what they do today, but only so long as it does not prevent them from also revering and believing in what they do tomorrow, regardless of how it might contradict. As Ralph Waldo Emerson said, "No man can antedate his experience, or guess what faculty or feeling a new object shall unlock, any more than he can draw today the face of a person whom he shall see tomorrow for the first time."

As long as there are more *tomorrows*, there will continue to be more faces to see and draw. And no single face should be revered ultimately or exclusively, but rather, the whole process of seeing new faces.

32

The past several times I've had an MRI, I've requested copies of the scans to take home. I have a decent collection now. I like having the chance to look at them while I'm by myself. It's hard to really make sense of and take in an image of your brain while in a doctor's office.

Sometimes I'll be at home, a couple whiskeys in, and just look at the scans, feeling the strangest sensation.

The whole image sort of looks like a mess to me. Regardless of the tumor. The fact that that's where I am—somewhere inside that mess—is beyond absurd. Of course, it's not as if I'm only recently realizing that I am inside my brain, but seeing images of your brain while still being in your brain really puts that strangeness into perspective. Something somewhere inside that image is trying to figure everything out. Trying to figure out itself, the world, the universe. While I look at the scans feeling and questioning this strangeness, I realize that, in real-time, the brain is contemplating how it is looking at itself from within itself, using methods derived from itself.

The idea, design, and construction of MRI machines are all derived from brains. And so, the brain has created machines to look at itself in an effort to understand, improve, and resolve issues of itself.

I find this both unbelievably impressive and unfathomably confusing. Which is to say, the brain finds its own abilities unbelievably impressive and unfathomably confusing.

33

The human brain appears to be a logical and linear perceptual tool. When measured on top of the universe, it perceives and measures for consistent, logical order. To some degree, it appears that the universe has corresponding qualities that line up with it. But at the same time, it also appears that it doesn't.

Just because a tool is put on top of something doesn't mean it accurately measures the entirety of the object that it's attempting to measure. If I put a ruler in a glass of water, I would accurately know how tall the water is, but that's just one, likely irrelevant, quality of the water. What I likely need to know is the volume or the temperature of the water, which I obviously won't be able to with the ruler. And even further, if my objective is to understand the water wholly, down to its molecular structure, I need significantly more information via many more tools.

What happens when you only have access to some of the tools necessary to understand the thing you're trying to understand fully in order to understand it at all?

You can't measure anything against itself. As far as I'm aware, nothing can ever do this and derive any meaning. We measure motion with time. Time with money. Money with objects. And so on. We measure everything against something else in order for any of it to mean anything.

For example, we can measure ten miles per hour, but we can't measure ten hours per hour, or ten hours per ten hours. At best, we can measure twenty-four hours per day or sixty minutes per hour, but that's not really measuring time itself. It's partitioning and comparing less of itself to more of itself, which isn't measuring. To measure time against itself, we would need to be able to do something like one second per second. But of course, the meaning here crumbles in on itself. It provides nothing.

And so, perhaps as part of the universe, humanity trying to measure itself against the universe elicits the same phenomenon. A crumbling of understanding. A nothingness. We are the inch trying to measure an inch. A second trying to measure a second. A universe trying to measure a universe. Nothing comes of itself other than itself. Because of this, the universe is chaos in the eyes of the human being. Because the eyes of the human being are made of the chaos that is universe.

We are not subject to or subject from the universe, we are of the universe. What sense does this make to our experience of self? Not much. And so, we struggle and squirm.

34

I watched a movie today. I cried maybe four times. Sometimes the crying overlapped with laughing.

I sat with myself for a while after it ended. It's been hard to do much else, and sometimes between watching movies, writing, and reading, I prefer to just do nothing other than think.

I thought about the film for a while. Then I thought about film in general. I thought about how and why people love to watch films so much.

Throughout my life, and still to this very moment, I have always found myself questioning the validity and reality of my self, my will, and my perception. Everything I perceive and hope to be real could merely be a fragile, false illusion. And I've always had that anxiety in the background of things. But just like a film, as long as we perceive it as *real*, it's real enough. Enough to enjoy. Enough to cry and laugh over. Enough to invest in and reap the benefits of.

We like films not because they're *real*, but because they're so good at creating the illusion of real. The illusion of experience. And during every good film, we don't know how much is real, where anything exactly came from, what everything precisely means, nor how it will end. And as soon as we do, arguably, the film becomes spoiled. And we become upset that it becomes spoiled, even though it isn't real.

35

Perhaps the human condition exists in a period of conscious evolution in which consciousness is evolved enough to care about the meaning of itself, but not evolved enough to know what it is. In this exists a perfect balance of awareness and unawareness. Ability and inability. Intelligence and ignorance. A tragically beautiful intersection.

A lizard doesn't know the meaning of life because it doesn't have the capacity to care. Some distant future being that operates from some super-intelligence might know the meaning of life, but also won't likely have the capacity to care, seeing as it would no longer have any interest or need to care now that it knows.

Perhaps to be human is to struggle one's whole life to find some solid ground to stand on and then die never coming anywhere close. And perhaps that's not even a *bad thing*. To know the true meaning of life and self is to do what with it? End the mystery? End the game? What then?

Perhaps one day we will find some unifying theory of everything and perhaps somehow this will make everything better. But what are the odds that we still care about the point of life after we've found it?

Imagine a movie in which you knew exactly why and what everything was from the start.

Imagine a life.

If we found a theory of everything or equation that connected the mysteries of quantum mechanics and Einstein's Theory of General Relativity, and we understood the very core of how and why the universe worked, what difference would this really make in terms of the meaning of life? Would two different people still not watch the same movie and experience and interpret two different things? We would, of course, all agree that it's a movie and on how the movie works, but when it comes to meaning, there will always remain a perceptual layer completely relative to the individuals observing it. Because of this, if we found the overarching, ultimate truth of existence tomorrow, half of the world would not believe it. The other half would fight for it. And as a whole, we would be no different. And if somehow the whole world did agree upon one truth, what then? Utopia? What then?

Utopia is an antonym for the human condition. If utopia existed, humanity would not be the creator nor the experiencer of it. At least not in the form that human seems to exist now.

Perhaps we evolve into some over-human; a super-intelligent being. And perhaps some utopic condition of the world and universe at large is created. But it will not be humans in charge anymore if humanity is still in existence at all. Humanity does not appear to possess the required intelligence and unity and oversight for such an ideal. And even if humanity does and is still in existence during a time of utopia, no one alive now will be alive then. So what use does this hope even have for existing now?

The truth we seek when considering the quality and meaning of our lives is not an outward truth. Not a truth that resolves the questions of the universe. But a truth that gleans inward and assembles into a stable self that can be integrated seamlessly into our perception of the whole around us. A truth we can't ever truly have. Truth is not even the right word here. There is no right word here. That's the point.

I sit here writing. Thinking about my being. About the strange relationship I have with this life and this plane of existence. I think about how alive I feel right now while writing; how potent this moment is; how insane and beautiful it is; how important it has been to me in the past; thinking, writing, talking, and reading about earnest experiences and attempts at living. Personally, the direct confrontation with the challenges, complexities, sufferings, and plights of the human condition have provided me with some of, if not all of the most profound, potent, and beautiful moments of my life. And I wonder if I would have ever experienced any of those undeniably worthy moments if life made sense? If it didn't hurt and overwhelm me? How beautiful would the night sky be if we knew exactly where it went and how the stars got there? How incredible would a view from a mountain top be if we knew exactly why the rocks and trees were the way they were? Would we ever be inspired to create art and form interpretations out of this life? What would I have written about? What would I have read about? How would I have ever found love or friendship or connection with others? Why would I have ever laughed or cried? What would I be doing right now? Would there be anything to say? Anything to live or die for?

I don't feel that my life would have been any better if I had known any more of what it was all about. In fact, I think it would have only worsened the whole thing.

We seem to so desire certainty. An immortality. A utopic end to conflict, suffering, and misunderstanding. And yet, in the final elimination of all darkness exists light with no contrast. And where there is no contrast of light, there is no perception of light at all.

What we think we want is rarely what we do. If we ever got what we did, we would no longer have anything. What we really want is to want. To have something to ceaselessly chase and move towards. To feel the motion and synchronicity with the universe's unending forward movement.

Like how all great relationships and friendships are comprised of two people who counterbalance one another through various intricate, oppositional forces and traits, so too does the human exist in relationship with the universe.

The relationship between us and the universe must persist with a counterbalance. A confrontation. A give and take. A rational faced with the absurd. A meaning faced with a meaninglessness. The finite faced with the infinite.

Like most relationships, it has its rather intense ups and downs and we have our differences, but we stay in the relationship because, inside us both, for some reason we still want each other.

36

How little we know about what we think we are working towards. The straight-A student may know how to answer all of the questions on the test but he or she has no better idea as to why such a test fundamentally exists in the first place than the student who forgot to show up that day. Similarly, the successful, important, or wise person knows no more about why they or anything fundamentally *is* than the person that was never born.

We are just as wise as the gods we created and just as clueless as the insects we smack down from our walls. We are just as insignificant as the dirt we walk on and just as marvelous as the cosmic nebulas that float above us. We are part of the whole of nature, cluelessly embedded in everything.

The only difference between, for example, a human and a tree is that the human is aware that it is or isn't called a tree and isn't phenomenally perceived as one. However, this awareness does not change the fact that, in essence, the human is not fundamentally any different than a tree. A tree emerges the same way a human does. A sequence of change and evolution across a vast, unknown, and unchosen order of flux, all a part of a singular whole of what we call nature. We feel as though we are not nature because we observe nature and call nature "nature." But of course, this is just nature calling itself "nature."

If there were no trees, there would be no humans. How could one suggest, then, that trees are not an equal part vital organ of the whole that human is associated? As Alan Watts would say, we are not organisms in an environment, we are organisms and an environment. An organism-environment.

37

Of course, no one chose all of *this*. It happened onto us unwillingly. Every generation was injected with a reproductive force and will to life by the prior, all the way back to the microbes and beyond. An unending sequence of forced being and willingness. No one, not even the collective body of humanity, is in control of anything that is human. Human itself is just as much not human as human.

We are all, in essence, passengers in this game of evolutionary experimentation. We could all be aggressively and competitively working towards something worse than this or indifferent to us. Or perhaps not. At a minimum, it's something we are cluelessly lost in.

We all run around in a panic, horrified that we aren't enough. We scream at and hate each other over this and that. We avert and destroy our own selves. We sabotage and betray those we love. We kill and get killed for reasons we don't understand. We make great efforts towards nothing. If one needs any proof that we have no idea what we are doing and that no one is in control, it is this.

38

Imagine for a moment that we are the apes that came before us, evolving through time and space. Then some sub-human species emerges out of us. Then that sub-human species evolves further and further until, sometime in the distant future, it becomes humanity—us right now—ruling the world. As essentially unconscious beings, the apes fought with each other and with the world in order to selectively survive and reproduce, facilitating the evolution of themselves without even knowing why or what was happening at all. And now, here we are. And there they are. Some of which are in zoos.

If we evolved out of them, something will be evolving out of us. And that is what we are likely moving towards.

Unlike any other species before us, though, we are consciously observing the evolution of our self out of our self. We still remain unaware of what we are doing and why, not dissimilar from the apes and anything that led to us before them, but we do experience the unique difference of self-reflection, rational consideration, and potential temperance. What does this mean for our future and the future direction of evolution? Perhaps nothing. Perhaps a lot.

Perhaps the sense of conscious reflection is merely just another instrument created by the cold indifference of evolution, no more than an illusory experience given to humanity to use against itself for the purpose of evolution. Or perhaps we hold some part of the reins now.

39

A couple of friends and I were talking the other day, and one of them—more of a friend of a friend—brought up the topic of *legacy* or *impact*. He asked me if I was happy with mine—or what mine will be. In summary, I said I'm not sure. Admittedly, I've been thinking a little about what the effects of my life might look like after I'm gone and whether or not they'll be generally *good*, but my only real, continued conclusion is that I am not sure.

Ultimately, no matter how much we might like to try to imagine the answers to these questions, in truth, we have no idea what the world or humanity really needs. Both on the large, collective scale and on the minute, individual scale.

How could a being know what anything else needs if that same being doesn't even know who they themselves really are and what they themselves really need?

It's popular to claim that one wants to change the world. Or to claim that one is; that they are "making the world a better place." I would concede that there's nothing inherently wrong with wanting to change the world—big or small—and that wanting to make it a better place is a *nice* thing. I think if anything is worth attempting to do in the blindness of this life, it is that. However, in truth, every day we get out of bed, cross a street, or say a single word to someone, we open the door to potentially changing the world forever. The most minute actions and happenings can cause the most impressive and massive changes thereafter, even when one isn't trying. No one can ever know the full scope of what their actions cause nor the net value of their so-called good or bad qualities. The reverberations of every action continue on beyond anyone's ability to discern them. And so, by the same token, when someone is trying to change the world—trying in the most noble and well-intended way—they have no real idea what they might be causing.

We are all going to change the world in some way or another. It doesn't hurt to try to do so for the better. But it's absurd and conceited to think that one can know if they ultimately are. If we wish to be honest with ourselves, we must recognize that we will never know for sure if our impacts actually make the world better or worse or neither. And that we will never be more or less important than anything else. No more than a deer that jumped out in front of a car and delayed the driver who, if he or she had been on time, would have caused a sequence of major world-changing events by influencing a different decision or action at the place they were going.

To want to change the world and make it better is truly the best use of the seemingly inevitable *selfish* programming of the human mind. It is as beautiful as it gets. But at the same time, I think if one is to truly derive any beauty from it, it shouldn't and can't be from whether or not one is successful in doing so, but rather, how well one truly means it. In other words, how well one recognizes that sometimes the most beautiful things are things that are never seen. That it's not about the accolades of being someone who made the world a better place. It's about someone who sincerely tried, which sometimes means doing less and being *no one*. Just being decent and kind and trying to help with the tentative humility that sometimes you can't.

Ultimately, there is something far beyond our control and sight taking place around and through us. Our efforts to change the world are themselves motivated by something; some force beyond our will and understanding. The same force that caused most of the things that are now problems we are trying to reverse. After all, much of the change that the world needs now is to merely offset the changes we thought the world needed before.

There is a movement in this world, random, patterned, or a mix of both that carries itself out with and through us. Some *thing* that we cannot outsmart or topple because we ourselves are it. If this is true, it is not toppling it that makes the world a better place, but perhaps acting in a way that respects that we are all a part of something that we can't seem to topple.

CHAPTER 6:
THE HOPE OF PESSIMISM

40

Living in a body sometimes feels like I'm trying to get comfortable in an uncomfortable couch. But can never get up from it.

I realized recently that I spend a lot of time just trying to get comfortable. I've been going from hospital bed to hospital bed; hospital chair to hospital chair; strange treatment machines to my own couch, bed, and everywhere in between. Everything is uncomfortable. The chairs and beds. All temperatures and places. Mostly all my clothes. But of course, it's none of those things. It's me. It's my body. My consciousness. For some reason, they refuse to ever be comfortable. And I can never get out of them. I can only try to find a softer couch. Or change clothes. Or change the temperature. Or go somewhere else. And so on. All to only want the opposite nearly as soon as I feel any sliver of comfort in the change.

I think, at the risk of taking a little physical discomfort too far, it's this same mechanism that causes the constant dissatisfaction and discomfort in one's life in general. The constant yearning for more or something else. The insatiable desire for what you don't or can't have. The seemingly impossible ability to ever fully be comfortable with one's self and where you are.

We exist in the gears of life's operation, constantly churned and taunted with the moments in which the gears briefly open up to give us a second to breathe, only to crunch us back down into another continued rotation of discomfort and dissatisfaction.

41

You spend your whole life meandering around, hoping that it isn't all for nothing, knowing that it almost certainly is, just to die and never end up knowing for sure if you're right or not. I can't say for sure if I'm right or not here either; I can't even know if I'm right about knowing I can't know I'm right. And all worldly reason points only to the likeliness that I won't ever know.

42

I got fairly drunk last night. To the point where I didn't notice the taste or sting of a long swig of vodka. Not to the point where I didn't remember noticing it.

I was by myself. I've always drank. Often by myself. I'm technically not supposed to drink more than a moderate amount because of the chemotherapy and medications, but I'm not on any really serious conflicting medications right now, and at this point, if the risk is minimal, it's worth it.

When I was a young boy, I always thought people that drank were dumb. Then I got drunk for the first time. I guess I'm either dumb now or I was dumb then. Or more likely both.

It never really became a problem for me. At a certain point, drinking becomes a part of your routine and it carries a certain value in the equation of your week. But if you're as pragmatic and paranoid as I am, the same pragmatism and paranoia that drives you to drink keeps you from ever really crossing the line and drinking *too* much.

I remember one time at a party I was talking with one of my friends and a couple other people I didn't know. We were talking about getting drunk and I said something along the lines of, "I think the appeal of getting drunk is that it's like being dead. And we all want to be dead without having to die." The conversation went abruptly quiet and my close friend, probably out of some inability to know how to best carry on the conversation from there, said something like, "Jesus Christ, man," with a quick, shallow exhale to allude to some sort of surprise or discomfort, like I said something wrong. But I don't think it was wrong in the sense that they didn't agree, but wrong in the sense that what I said is likely pretty true, but it was a fucked-up thing to say.

In any case, I think it is true. At least at times, mostly everyone wants to be dead without having to die. Perhaps more accurately, mostly everyone wants to be asleep or knocked out of their normal head, without losing their normal, waking head to return to. And being drunk or high is perhaps one of the easier ways of doing this; sort of temporarily killing yourself.

It's as if life is like going on a painstakingly long road trip to nowhere, and when you get drunk, you're still on the road trip, but you get to switch from the driver's seat to the passenger's seat and more or less enjoy the view for a little while. You're often still giving directions, but you're finally able to relax a little and feel somewhat less responsible for where you're going and how.

Perhaps it was best said by one of the more notable *professional alcoholics*, Charles Bukowski. "When you drank the world was still out there, but for the moment it didn't have you by the throat."

Not all drinking takes it here; to the sort of fringe of consciousness. Most reasonable, healthy drinking doesn't. But most good drinking does. Even the hangovers, although indescribably dreadful, have always brought some cadence into my life that I have valued. A tiredness or fogginess that, like the drunkenness, almost helped sustain a certain balance of my soberness.

What is it about writers and drinking? I'm not sure. It does appear to be some sort of a mythology, though. Perhaps a self-fulfilling one.

Why do baseball players like chewing tobacco? Is it because people who like baseball also happen to be the same people who like chewing tobacco? Or is it because somehow, for some reason, it became a *thing*? One or a couple players who were worthy of idolization otherwise did it, and then those who idolized them did it, some of which became worthy of idolization themselves. And the cycle continued, developing into some ethos of the baseball player. Perhaps it's a mix wherein people who happen to like one also tend to like the other and then the whole thing is only compounded through circular influence. In any case, every identity group tends to form its own arbitrary *thing* or *things*. Drinking is one of writing's, I guess.

Ultimately, do I believe drinking is a good thing? Not really. I don't know what it is in terms of a good or bad thing. I don't think I would want my kid, if I had one, to drink all that much. But I don't know what that means either. I wouldn't want my kid doing a lot of what I've done, and yet many of those things I keep doing.

There's a cognitive dissonance that exists in so many of my actions, thoughts, and beliefs. Even to acknowledge the problems of my cognitive dissonance and do nothing about it is some sort of cognitive dissonance.

Life is a dissonance. There are times when there are two or more answers to the same question that are equally right and equally wrong, depending on what way you're *looking*. But in some of these cases, there's no right or wrong way of looking. To answer what way you should be looking only lends itself to the same phenomenon.

At bottom, it isn't clear what anyone should or shouldn't do. It seems to all depend on what one calibrates their life and self on. For example, it's fair to say that for anyone who wants to live, they shouldn't jump out of an airplane without a parachute. But what about for those who don't want to live? The same choice and action can have two dramatically different values of *right or wrong* depending on desire and intention. Not referring to any moral argument, but just in reference to one's self, whether one should live or die has no clear answer. And consequently, nor is how one should go about either.

At a certain point, within the limits of social morality, everyone has to do what they have to do to get by. Sometimes that means drinking. Sometimes that means staying far away from drinking. Sometimes that means running every morning. Sometimes that means watching your favorite TV show each night. Ultimately, one has to know themselves and where value meets deficit. Where escape lends itself to a degradation of the whole of which they inevitably must return.

Admittedly, it's sometimes—often times—nearly impossible to do this. To know when or if you're approaching the limit of a vice, or if the vice you're in is destined to destroy you. Some people get lucky. Some other huge percentage of people don't. There's a world filled with alcoholics and addicts of every possible kind; drug, TV, technology, food, sex, and all the rest. We all want to escape the standard norm of looping anxiety and boredom; the self. And some of us seem to get to without losing the self we are trying to escape. Some of us don't. And some of us die in the process of finding out.

There is great risk in everything in life and everything that tries to escape or survive it. Ultimately, it is all futile. You can't really escape. Not even through death itself.

43

In an instant, for any number of reasons, life can become very clear and meaningful. And then, in what almost seems like the same amount of time, it can lose all reason and comfort.

44

One day you wake up with the life you always wanted. Everything you dreamed of and imagined as a young child, adolescent, or full-grown adult. And you don't want to get out of bed.

45

Every morning I get up and I'm tired. And this isn't just because of the medications or treatments. I mean, in part it is. But it's also mostly just how it's always been. It's as if the whole point of sleeping for six to eight hours is lost within the seconds of waking up.

Getting ready to exist, waking up into this life, this reality, this self, is almost impossible. Every morning is a reawakening into the nightmare I fell asleep from. And yet, I always get up.

I think mostly everyone experiences this. At least to some extent. Even the so-called *morning people*. Even those people feel the weight of their existential *responsibility* drop onto their chest as soon as their eyelids open for the first time in the morning. It's like that for me at least. There seems to be a string attached to my eyelids that, when opened, releases the weight of the world onto my torso.

In my view, it's often an act of rebellion to get up in the morning; a revolt against everything that is obviously worth staying in bed for. The comfort and silence and numbness of the bed compared to the chaos and absurdity of the world. But despite the often-good reasons to prefer staying in bed, I still get up. Everyday. Mostly everyone does. We still have a world that mostly shows up on time every day. And if that isn't a powerful testament to something, I don't know what is. Whether it's a testament to our foolishness, our fortitude, or both, is unclear. But it's a damn near wonder for sure.

46

We are the universe observing itself. This sounds beautiful. Plenty of fantastic quotes have been made from this sentiment; perhaps even some by me. But it's not so beautiful if the universe is hell. But perhaps even hell has its appeal.

47

We've wanted order, happiness, perfection and so on for as long as humans have had the luxury of considering such terms. And yet, although the world has improved in many ways, in other fundamental ways, it hasn't changed much at all. The fundamental existential sufferings of humankind have seemed only to mutate and take different forms. The anxiety and depression of being. The sensitivity to life's confusion and absurdity. The vulnerability to tragedy, crisis, and so on. The tension between identity groups. The lack of human connection and understanding. Despite any and all of the inconceivably impressive developments on the surface of society, these have gone nowhere and, in many cases, seem to have become worse.

Life carries inevitable suffering. And life always finds its way. Like trying to climb a mountain to get away from our self, we go with us, up and down the mountain. Wherever we go. When we think we can beat the game by disregarding its rules—when we assume that we are of some innate, higher importance than nature, as if we are special and the universe is set up to serve us rather than itself—we only fuel the suffering of our existence.

Arguably, to imagine and desire a future in which happiness will somehow rain down from the heavens and nothing will ever hurt or feel strange or confusing or scary—this is the strangest, scariest, and most confusing thing one could ever do to themselves. It sets one up for horrible, consistent catastrophe, disillusionment, and disappointment.

At some point, if desperate enough, one will have thought of and tried everything that was supposed to make everything *all good*, happy, easy, or peaceful. And then, one will have to realize that everything isn't *all good*, happy, easy, or peaceful. And so, if anything is going to be *good*, it has to be that things aren't always so.

As long as one is alive, they will be restricted to the conditions of life. And so the solution, if there is one, must subvert the very intention of even needing to find one to begin with. A paradoxical approach in which the solution to the problem comes when you stop trying to solve it. The solution to life, then, is perhaps not a *solution* at all, but the absence of needing a one.

48

Life is an equation multiplied by zero. No matter what you add to it and how big you make it, you still end up with zero.

We will all lose everyone we love, whether it's them or us first.

We will fight for our need for certainty and control, and the universe will throw its indifference and chaos back at us. We will do a bunch of stuff to make the world a better place and fuck it up worse. We will do everything right and still feel scared, confused, wrong, and unhappy. We will never find ultimate solace in any place, person, thing, idea, or way of life. We will exist on the edge of madness. We will flail around in the turbine of boredom and anxiety. Everything we've ever done will dissolve away with us, and if somehow there is anything left in some remote, distant future, the universe will swallow it with its last meal.

Can we still be okay, though? Can we still be okay in spite of all this and more?

We have no other choice.

It might be considered negative or pessimistic to discuss matters in some of the ways I have done here. Throughout my life, I certainly erred on that side of the spectrum. But is it not all the more pessimistic to pretend these matters aren't true? To play ignorance towards these real thoughts, feelings, and potential facts of life? To pretend that what is real is not, or to ignore it, is to suggest that one is incapable of handling the truth of their existence. That they are too weak and must look the other way. That, to me, is far more pessimistic. It's hopelessness, really.

Arguably, only when one confronts and makes their most honest attempt at truth, at least as they see it, can one have any chance at surviving who they really are and what life might really be.

If I feel that life is fundamentally suffering, would it make me more or less hopeless in stating that I feel this way? By admitting it—by saying it and continuing to live—I am, in all actuality, exhibiting a hope. An optimism that I can know this truth and be okay in spite of it.

On the contrary, if I feel a constant suffering in life but state that I do not, I am actually exhibiting a hopelessness by acting as if I am incapable of surviving my own condition and must deny what I feel and know to be *real*. My own intelligence. My own truth. Instead of facing myself and my reality, I would be turning around and running the other way towards contrived, impossible ignorance. To not face one's self and the tumultuous reality they are born into—that is hopelessness, not optimism. To face it and be as honest as possible with it—that is a resolute form of true optimism, if there is any.

Albert Camus discussed this in his notion of the *revolt*. To know of the absurd meaninglessness of everything and the fate and plight of man but to refuse to be broken by it. To still fight against it. To still live in spite of it. To still create meaning and choice out of everything, even in the futility and perhaps delusion of everything.

True wisdom is not found in the realization of life's potential bleakness, but in the response to it. To know of how little one can know of the absurdity that pains them, and to choose to keep living anyway. It is in this that the true essence and uniqueness of the human spirit emerges. To refuse to give in to the obvious hopelessness. And to find hope somewhere in the hopelessness, nonetheless.

The only thing more absurd than to hope for the impossible is to continue to live without any kind of hope at all.

I believe that there is a *hope* in hopelessness. A subversive type that desires and feeds on the suffering of life, even when one has surrendered all rational hope. I recognize this when I see that even in the pains and horrible treatments of my final illness, I have not killed myself and I have no desire to. Every day I don't and haven't throughout my whole life, I exhibited a spirit of life that persists in spite of my intelligence and pragmatism. An innate desire to live and continue beyond any conscious understanding or reason.

Arguably, every human being over the age of twelve who hasn't committed suicide is a living embodiment of one of two things: this form of hope or some form of fear. Hope that life is worth living in spite of its conditions. Or fear that the alternative is worse. But I would argue that even in the latter, if one's fear of death outweighs the desire to kill themselves, they are nonetheless still embodying a spirit of hopefulness. Hopefulness might not be the right word, but it likely serves as closely to the purpose as any other word.

49

Whether life is worth living or not is perhaps the question of everything. Camus wrote, "There is but one truly serious philosophical problem, and that is suicide." Shakespeare wrote, "To be, or not to be: that is the question." Which is perhaps the most famous line in all of literature. It is this question—a question that has been uttered and conveyed in uncountable forms of literature, philosophy, science, technology, and art—that everything stands on. Because what can be worthwhile in life if life itself is not?

Personally, I believe the true tragedy of life is not that life isn't worth living, but that it is.

We are the only beings given the lens of conscious perception and the projector of rational understanding, and then forced to watch a movie that tears both apart. We are compelled to cling and fall in love with it; to try to will ourselves onto it; to feel like we are important to something in it; all only to control nothing and lose everything.

I am not sure if conscious life is a gift, a curse, or both. To love is to lose. To think and try is to fail. To live is to die. But is it better to have done all the above, than to have not? I think it's possible. But I also think that such a possibility creates the tragedy of life. That living and loving and trying can be so wonderous and potent and beautiful that they're all worth their inevitable, tragic doom. And that such an unbelievably high level of wondrousness creates an unfathomably tragic level of doom.

50

How can something so tragic be so beautiful? How can something so cruel be so fair? How can someone hate and love the same thing with all their being at the same time?

51

One can't say that everything is meaningless without this statement itself being meaningless. Thus, in an infinite regress, to even speak of life being meaningless is to give it meaning. One cannot speak of nothingness without ascribing somethingness to it. Humankind cannot escape the paradox of the meaning-creating machine that is itself. In every perception; in every act of thought—positive or negative; in every action—revolt or surrender; the human is giving meaning to the nothingness of life. It can't be escaped. And falling in love with it can't be avoided.

CHAPTER 7:
REGRET & SELF-LOATHING

52

All old and new methods of treatment have continued to help, but not significantly. The new radiation treatment has helped more than the prior, but again, not significantly. There is one other treatment process that my doctor mentioned that involves injecting a treatable virus into the surrounding brain cavity, which then ends up inside the tumor, latching onto the cancer cells. After this, I would then take a medication designed to target and treat the virus, theoretically killing the virus and subsequently, the cancer cells too. This supposedly has shown some interesting, positive results in other patients.

I applied two weeks ago for the treatment, but because of the specifics of my current condition and the other prior treatments I've undergone, I don't qualify.

The tumor isn't entirely inoperable yet though, so I have another standard surgery on Friday of this week.

53

Imagine I told someone right now that I was going to take their parents, friends, lovers, kids, all their possessions, their career, their status, everything they've ever worked for, their ability to see, hear, smell, taste walk, talk, move, think, and anything else I might have missed. It would be the most unfathomably devastating news ever imagined. And yet it's all of our fates.

54

We all know it could all end tomorrow. And we all know that if it did, on some level, we would be upset with how we lived today. And yet, we keep living each today mostly the same. And perhaps we live today even worse because of this whole awareness.

My whole life, I worried about regretting my life. And this very foresight concern of regret made my life more regrettable. It made me careful about everything, never able to do or say the things I wanted. It made me hedge the unending present moment for the imagined tomorrow.

Why is it that knowing your life will end but not knowing when makes you feel like you don't need to do or say the things you want to do and say? It's as if the uncertainty of the end of life imposes some mirage effect on the conscious mind, which convinces you that you have forever. That if every day, I still have tomorrow, I have all the *tomorrows* in the world.

I lived like this. And then, of course, I started running out of tomorrows.

55

I ended up having two surgeries back to back. After three days of recovering in the hospital from the first regularly scheduled surgery, it was deemed that another surgery should be conducted immediately while I was still there. Apparently what they did the first time around didn't quite suffice, and it was only clear a couple days after. I don't know. I don't really understand what's happening anymore. At a certain point, I gave up trying to really understand it. I follow along and do what I have to do, but ultimately, when doctors who have dedicated their entire life to understanding and treating such a condition can't really understand or resolve anything, I don't stand a chance.

There was a moment around the initial diagnosis when I considered sort of immersing myself into researching the entirety of my situation. The anatomy of the brain, cancer in general, brain tumors of my type, and so on. But with the odds becoming really only about how long I live and not whether or not I do, I decided I'd rather just spend my time not doing that.

I'd prefer to just read and write and talk about anything else.

In any case, the second surgery went better. Whatever that means. I suppose it means I have a little more time.

56

My mom has been coming over somewhat frequently. Maybe once or twice a week. She's been helping me after my surgeries and coming with me to some of my doctor and treatment appointments in general. She has been trying to help me through this whole thing as much as she can.

My dad passed away several years ago. I haven't had a girlfriend in about a year and a half and the girls I've been with since were not in it for the brain-tumor-long-haul. My remaining friends help here and there if there's anything they can do, but I mostly don't let them. I am unnecessarily prideful. Always have been. My mom is the only one around who I'll kind of let help. And barely, at that.

Today I had an appointment with another new doctor who is supposed to start helping with better pain management. My mom asked me if I wanted her to come. I mostly didn't. But I said yes anyway. Partly because I knew she wanted to, and partly because I think, somewhere in me, I did want her there.

After the appointment, she drove me back and essentially invited herself in to help with miscellaneous stuff around the house.

The whole day, before, during, and after the appointment, I was generally annoyed. For one, I've always been impatient and miserable to some degree. And dying and dealing with doctors' appointments and surgeries and treatments and regret and all the rest doesn't help. But for two, I was annoyed with my mom. I think mostly just because I was already upset and annoyed and she was there to be annoyed at. But also because of the sort mother-son back-and-forth that can occur when your mom tries to help, but you don't really want her to, and the help almost feels like an insult or degradation. The sort of immature back-and-forth that forms as a young child or teenager and never quite fully shakes until your much older, if at all.

I wasn't just annoyed internally. I would imagine I was clearly annoyed and showing it. I was impatient, closed off, and harsh. I don't really want her help, even if I could use it and would probably want it if she stopped. But because she pushes it onto me, it often becomes hard to appreciate. And the worst part is I'm aware of how foolish and awful it is to be annoyed at someone for wanting to help you. But this only makes me more annoyed and frustrated. I know I should, at a minimum, be decent to be around for someone who cares and is trying to help. And more likely, I should be very happy and appreciative. But when you're some amount miserable, it becomes hard to just act in the way you want. To understand and forgive. To smile and appreciate. To exhibit patience and calmness. And the worst part is, the sort of misery and self-hatred that causes your negative behaviors is only further fueled by them.

I'll be in some miserable, self-loathing mood, then my mom or someone will do something slightly off, which will make me mad and impatient towards her, which will then make me loathe myself more for being mad at someone who's innocent or just trying to help. It's a vicious cycle.

On paper, you would think that self-hatred would make you want to avoid focusing on yourself, but self-hatred is just another version of self-interest. It makes you incapable of properly caring or being aware of anyone else other than yourself. When you're miserable, you convince yourself that mostly everything you do is excusable, or at least understandable. In your mind, you're the victim. But in reality, you're the causer and spreader of more misery.

This whole thing affects my mom too. My dad passed when I

was twenty-five. My mom's dad passed before I was born when she was twenty-two. Her mom passed a few years ago. She has a mother-in-law and two brothers left, along with their families. I'm her only child.

When I die, she'll sort of be by herself.

Honestly, if anyone is getting the worst of this situation, it's her. And yet, she has to play Mom while I play victim.

I truly do appreciate her and her help more than I can even know and express. And I believe that she knows that. But I also believe that she deserves to hear and see it more.

57

When my dad died, I felt like I never really got to say what I wanted to say or ask him what I wanted to ask him. His death was abrupt. And by the time we realized he was going to pass, he could barely talk.

In truth, I don't think I ever really knew who he was. Not on any real, holistic level at least. Sure, there were moments when I could see who he likely really was peering out, and of course everyone has an implicit understanding of their parents, but beyond these little flash moments and general, vague senses, I never really knew him. At least I never knew for sure if I did. I certainly never knew what he thought about life and death. What he thought about God or the lack thereof. What he thought about love and friendship and misery. I never knew many details or stories of his life.

Despite this, though, I still always felt fairly close with him. We mostly knew where we stood, what we meant, and how we generally thought through small, subtle actions and statements. But I was always, and still am, more curious about who he *really* was. It's weird to think that someone you were close with your whole life, you only knew a little bit about in just one context of theirs.

Ever since he passed, I often catch myself with a problem or a thought that I need to share or ask someone. Someone that could only possibly be him. I'll have the sudden impulse to call him followed by the seemingly even more sudden realization that I can't. Then I'll have the sudden desire to tell him how much I appreciate and miss him, again followed by the realization that I can't.

58

Love, to some degree, is learned like anything else. How one accepts, invites, and shows affection and appreciation is acquired from those who gave it to them as a child.

I rather loathe the sentimental or showy type of love and appreciation. I wasn't raised on that kind. And frankly, I'm happy about that. Maybe that's a downfall for me in certain areas. Probably one of the sources of some of the problems in many of my past relationships. It's not as if there's no love in me, but it's a love that is contained in a shell, no less valuable and no less present, but always sanctioned off by a thin layer of an easily breakable, yet constantly rigid façade. Like an egg. Because of that, I struggle to fully show or speak of my love and appreciation for the things and people I love and appreciate. I think for some people, like my dad and myself, that sort of stuff only makes one uncomfortable. And so, him and I and the vast number of other people like us always interact from a distance.

Personally, I think implicit, unspoken love can be just as potent and meaningful as spoken, explicit love. In even the smallest, unloving actions, love can still be known and felt. And I think everyone on the same page mostly knows what's written on the page. Of course, though, sometimes not everyone is on the same page. And sometimes it can become unclear as to which page everyone is on and what everyone knows, seeing as how it's never really spoken.

Sometimes it might be worth breaking the eggshell open. Even if it feels weird. Feeling weird is vastly better than feeling too late.

Even though I think my dad and grandfather and all my friends and past girlfriends that I've lost through life or death all knew how we felt, I think there were somethings I could have done and said a little more clearly. At least once in a while. I don't know. Maybe it would have just ruined how nice things already were. I'd like to think it wouldn't have.

59

I had an appointment earlier this week on Monday. MRI scans showed the tumor has mostly grown back. It's starting to spread further in and around other parts of my brain. The last real opportunities to manually do anything about it have passed and I am approaching what will likely be the final stages of everything.

Following the appointment, I have spent most of my days mainly thinking about my life and regretting things. Hating myself. Getting upset. Getting upset at myself for getting upset. Trying to rationalize the process of my death and the pitfalls of myself. And then repeat. Which is to say, as I've become more aware of the even less time I have left, I've spent that time regretting, only to create more suffering to loathe and regret.

Even when I realized this, I mostly continued doing it.

It's a vicious and perhaps inescapable cycle. You become upset by something you can't control or can control but are doing the opposite of what you know you should, and then you realize how insane, absurd, and insufferable you're being by acting or thinking in such a way. And then you dip into self-hatred and self-loathing for acting so foolish, which then makes you feel even more insane and detestable knowing that instead of just feeling better or being better, you've figured out how to push yourself further away from any chance of doing so, which more or less starts the whole cycle over. This isn't exclusive to me now. I've realized that it's sort of what I've always done. But it's much easier to notice and put into words when it's taken to such an extreme.

CHAPTER 8:
COMING TO TERMS WITH CHOICES I NEVER CHOSE

60

I've mostly always known what to do in order to live as best I could. I've mostly known how to think about things so to help me feel and see things better. I've known that there is a good part of life to be *happy* about. I've known that there is a sublime to be touched. I've known life's potentially beautiful and joyful moments when I've seen and been in them. And yet, I have not done much of any of it. I have not enjoyed nor appreciated more than a small fraction of the moments that were worthy of enjoying and appreciating. I rarely ever fully synced up with what I knew I should have done and how I should have thought. I would always deceive or sabotage myself in the process.

I've overcome a great number of specific problems, fears, and anxieties, but I've never overcome problems, fears, and anxieties in general. As clever as I've gotten at resolving my problems, I seemed to have gotten equally clever at creating or sustaining them.

I accept humanity's chief distinctive quality to be rationality. But what rational being in control of themselves would choose to not love, smooth over, enjoy, and appreciate every reasonably enjoyable moment? What kind of being hates themselves or brings suffering onto themselves knowing that hating themselves and suffering makes them miserable? Perhaps a being that is far more than what it can begin to feel and know. A being whose *self* operates on levels both out of its control and beyond its awareness.

Who am I to say which part of me is the one that self-sabotages me? Who is the *I* saying anything here? Is the part that fights with myself and keeps me from what *I want* less me? More me? Or equally me?

We operate on the surface of our self, atop the deep sea that is our entire being. A rational observer floating above the entire sub-self that exists underneath it. But the water on the bottom of the ocean is no less part of the ocean than the water on the top, even if the top is all you really seem to see.

It is all part of the same whole. Every conscious choice or thought I've ever made or had was equally some part unconscious. The thing inside my head—the eye or voice or whatever else—was just observing and working with what it had access to, mostly always thinking it was in control and running the show, but mostly unaware and unable to see the thousands of feet of water below the surface.

I don't think I should have done anything differently, though.

I realize now that I was never my conscious self, but I was never my unconscious self either. Just like I was never my heart or my hand or anything else on its own. I was never even solely what is contained inside my brain or body. I am everything, in and out. I am not separate from everything I observe. I am everything I observe; a passenger to nature given a false sense of ultimate control like an infant child given a fake steering wheel in the back seat of a moving car so that they can feel like they are driving.

But this is not to say that as part of this whole of nature—as passenger—I shouldn't have felt what I felt and done what I did. Even the child in the back seat with a steering wheel can distract or influence the real driver of the car, after all.

It's not that I didn't need to make every choice I made. It's not that I shouldn't have cared and tried deeply. It's not that I shouldn't have wanted to know and achieve my desired life of peace and control. And it's not that I shouldn't have gotten upset when I did the wrong things or when the wrong things happened. I needed to try my best in every moment and make every choice, right or wrong.

To live is to be in pursuit of something *impossible*. For life to sustain itself, it must keep going. And to keep going, there must be no end to the desires of that which carries it. Rather, it must be a relentless push and pull in the desire to find nothing.

We exist as a feature or tool of some apparently self-sustaining life substrate that operates in and through us. I am not the person who wants what's best for me. And by the same token, I am not the person who often causes all the problems that keep me from what's best for me. I am both, fighting against each other. My *self* arises out of this layering of push and pull; conflict and resolution; desire and impossibility. Without my constant pushing and pulling, there would be nothing at all. No self. Now show. No life.

We are all both the puppet and the puppeteer. If there was no such thing as a puppet, there would be no such thing as a puppeteer, and vice versa. They are two parts of the same whole of their existence. Every conscious entity is this. And as puppets contained by strings, we spend our lives pulling at them, creating tension, and making things worse by always trying to make things better. And as a result, we constantly feel and think we are weak, incapable, or foolish. But it is all part of the show.

My being came with strings. And my being came with a desire to pull at the strings. So what am I to do other than live with strings and pull at them?

I find sudden and unsurpassable relief in this thought. It's not bleak. It simply reveals that there is nothing to regret. I tried my best. The things I could've changed, I did. The things I couldn't, I didn't. And the things I didn't know I should've, I never thought to try. I was exactly who I could have been. Exactly who I needed to be. I did everything right by doing a great deal of things wrong. There is nothing to regret. I never had a choice.

I see this now.

61

If you live as if you'll die tomorrow, and you don't, you risk killing yourself today. If you live as if you won't die tomorrow, you risk never living today. We are stuck between knowing we could die at any moment but probably won't, and definitely dying at some point, but not knowing when. And in constantly being pulled from both sides, we often become inert.

What would I have done differently if I had known I would die this early? Maybe a lot. Maybe not that much. Ultimately, it doesn't matter. It didn't matter before I knew because I didn't know, and it doesn't matter now, when I do know, because I can't go back.

To spend a day fully risks losing what one has; wealth, love, safety, health, life itself. To conserve a day fully is to gain nothing of what one wants; wealth, love, excitement, wonder, life itself. To regret a day fully is to think that one knows how to reconcile and manage this balance.

62

The last couple days have been much better. Not good. But better.

63

There is no life without decisions. And there are few decisions without regret. Søren Kierkegaard wrote, "I see it all perfectly; there are two possible situations—one can either do this or that. My honest opinion and my friendly advice is this: do it or do not do it—you will regret both."

In nearly every decisive moment, however big or small, we come face-to-face with the infinite possibilities of who we can be and what we can do. And in this—in nearly every moment—we come face-to-face with the angst of impossible decisions and the foresight of their regret.

We will naturally always feel the desire to make the best possible choice. And will always feel the sense that we can or could have. That if one thing went this way instead of that way; if we had just a little more courage or a little more time; if we made just a little bit more of an intelligent decision or did something just a little bit differently; everything would have been better.

It is more likely that on the other side of every choice is a nearly equal quandary of dissatisfaction and regret.

Regret implies that there is a right choice that one could have made. But how could there be a right or wrong one if one can't ever know? We can never know what's on the other side of any decision we didn't make, that we wished we did. Furthermore, most decisions that are hard or regrettable are hard not because there is a right choice even in the case that one could see the future. Life *paths* often contain qualities impossible to discern as ultimately better or worse through any concrete value system, and so, even if one could see how the different choices played out, in certain cases, one would still likely struggle to know which is *right*.

The only thing one can know is that on the other side of every decision that doesn't kill them, they'll be there. And if they're anywhere, there'll always be something to dread and regret. Dread, angst, and some form of regret persist as symptoms of conscious life, infinite possibilities, a sense of choice, and hindsight. No decision or mode of life can remove such inevitable qualities of conscious human life, and thus, no life can exist without such a sense of angst and regret. But the paradox is that in this realization that regret is inescapable, regret loses much of its weight. To regret with the feeling that there could have been alternative ways of living and decision making that wouldn't have come with regret is to regret heavily. To regret with the awareness that no such life exists is to regret *lightly*. It is to essentially drain regret of much of its power.

And moreover, none of this even takes into account the strong debate against freewill, which only further places the notions of regret and self-sabotage and choice into the realm of absurdity.

I only wish I could have truly realized and felt this earlier. Maybe it wouldn't have mattered so much now.

CHAPTER 9:
THE PEACE IN DYING

64

It is perhaps both cliché and obvious to say that I've looked at things differently following and throughout the evolution of my diagnosis. But part of looking at things differently as death looms closer is caring less about whether or not things are cliché and obvious. Sometimes the most cliché and obvious things are the hardest to truly know anyway. That's often why they're cliché; because they're obvious, but we can't seem to get them through our skull.

There's a weird moment when you're doing something as simple and mundane as brushing your teeth, and you feel that cliché come to life. You become viscerally aware that at some point in the near future, you'll never brush your teeth and feel that feeling again. And it suddenly becomes a near-mystical experience. This goes for mostly anything. The feeling of a breath of air flowing in through the nostrils. The sensation of being thirsty followed by the sensation of water rushing down your throat. The feeling of being cold or hot or just right. The low humming sound of the refrigerator or air conditioner. The feeling of your heartbeat that you sometimes notice when you're lying in bed and can't fall asleep. The difficulty of getting out of bed. The pain you feel in the back of your neck when you're stressed. The look of light hitting your closed eyelids in different ways, making different blends and patterns inside them.

A simple, ordinary sunset. A simple, ordinary night sky. The touch of another person. The feeling of touching anything. Any blend of emotion, good or bad. Everything. You'll never experience any of it ever again, for all eternity. And suddenly, all the things you barely cared about—the things you barely even noticed—they become filled with a wealth that you would give anything to hold onto. And the cliché, archetypal experience of dying and seeing and appreciating life differently becomes real. So real and overwhelming that you finally actually feel why it appears in so many places. Because it really is that unfathomably potent, important, and sincere. And as a verbal construction, it means mostly nothing in comparison.

It's somehow both completely banal and completely insane to think that everything becomes nothing without you. Not necessarily nothing in the sense that everything outside of you is no longer there, but nothing in the sense that once you turn off, everything that has formed as a result of your unique conscious conception disappears forever. The particular version of everything that exists exclusively inside your head becomes nothing as your final brain wave washes it all away into oblivion.

On the other side of my skull is the world, the universe, everything, whatever it is. But for me, also on the other side of my skull is nothing. Without being inside my skull, there would be neither an inside nor an outside. It's only out of the contrasting relationship between my internal and external that any external exists at all. It's the same function of contrast that brings everything into *human experience*. Something can only be observed with an opposite something or point of neutrality to provide its distinction. Light and dark. Sound and silence. Cold and hot. Happiness and sadness. Deviation and normality. Observer and observed.

The very essence of being a conscious observer is itself birthed out of this same function of contrast with a counterpart. Something can only be observed with an observer, and an observer can only observe with something to observe. Without the other, there is neither. And so, in relation to conscious experience, everything is nothing without within. If there were no beings with internal realms and internal conceptions, there would be *nothing* external. Again, perhaps not literally nothing in the way we might think of absolute nothing, but perhaps a different kind of nothing; an *everythingness* all at once that becomes the same as nothing. The sort of nothing that one might describe as gibberish. If someone said something that means nothing in any language like, "Ska haglashuy hett ole eesh," we might say that they said nothing, which is true in the sense that they said nothing of any meaning, but untrue in that they literally said nothing. If we were to include in the definition of the word "said" the intention of uttering sounds to communicate, then one could argue that they did say something, but just nothing that means anything to anything else. This, although an extremely simplistic exemplification, is perhaps what might exist on the other side of every persons' skull. A flurry of matter and energy, unfathomably indiscernible, dancing and buzzing around, never in one spot, never in one form, never meaning anything other than itself, all beyond any conceivable subjectivity and objectivity. Or perhaps not.

At a certain point, the question becomes both impossible and irrelevant. In truth, no consciousness can know what it means to exist or perceive outside of consciousness. The same filter through which all conscious life is experienced is the same filter that keeps us from ever ultimately verifying anything outside of it.

Arguably, the most interesting part isn't even if anything is real in the way we might assume real to be, or how much anything is if it is, but the implication of the uncertainty. That through each person, some particular reality is perceived, understood, and created. And each deceased person carries it with them to the abyss; their everything, their particular conception and unique experience of reality that will never be known or experienced by anyone else.

Everyone says stuff like, "See, this is why you should appreciate what you have and not take anything for granted," whenever they observe something that doesn't affect them at all but is unimaginably horrible for someone else. But then, mostly everyone just goes back to not appreciating anything any differently within an hour or so. Perhaps not everyone is like this. And perhaps some people are better at *gratitude* or whatever you want to call it. But I know that's how I was; never truly able to sustain it for more than some small window of time. And it certainly seems like basically everyone else is like that too.

It's likely the same baseline that, at a certain point, keeps everyone essentially at the same level of happiness and misery no matter what they do. The hedonic treadmill. You don't get to be happy all the time and you don't get to be happier than your brain lets you. Just like you don't get to be grateful all the time or more appreciative of the little things than your brain lets you. And you don't actually know how much you're taking for granted until you're the person who's about to lose it all. Or the person who just did. It makes sense, really. But now, I'm the one. And I feel it for real. Like my threshold of awareness and appreciation has been recalibrated, and all the cliché and banal sentiments are real and true. I'm going to die soon and lose everything, and this is why you shouldn't take anything for granted. Why you should appreciate what you have while you have it.

Maybe there's hope for realizing this before you get to the point where it's nearly too late. And maybe it just requires a lot more effort than feeling it in one moment and then doing nothing about it. Maybe it's like any other skill, habit, aptitude, or exercise; constant and hard, but possible. Maybe not.

65

Our bodies and minds are mere rentals given to us by the universe for a vacation of conscious, physical existence, and at some point, they must be returned.

Being dead is not scary or undesirable. The conscious thought of dying while alive is.

Like a vacation to our favorite destination, we should try our best to not let our awareness of the trip's end-date ruin our vacation. Because ultimately, if a vacation went on forever, it wouldn't be a vacation at all.

Against all odds, we were given the opportunity to go on this vacation; to experience nature perceiving itself. And ironically, our fear of losing our ability to experience this is what can often ruin our experience of it.

I think this is what was responsible for a great measure of my disdain and inability to enjoy life. And I don't think I'm unique. I had the constant sense that just on the other side of me was nothing, and that I was, in every moment, hurdling towards this nothing; the end of the trip. And because of this, I struggled to just enjoy the trip while I was on it. How foolish. I was, in the most ironic way possible, sad about not being alive while I was alive.

66

When we talk of a coin, we describe it as one object with two sides. If each side is different, we can observe and consider what's different, but ultimately, one's understanding of either side only serves to constitute an understanding of the coin as a whole.

When we experience, consider, and discuss life, we also imply death. They are two sides of the same thing. However, since we can only consciously observe the one side of being, we are seemingly forced to believe that the whole coin of existence is just the one side we see; life. But it appears that life and death are just like everything else. Balance points and junctures of contrast. Neither of which could exist without the other. If we want life, then we also want death. Richard Dawkins said, "We are going to die, and that makes us the lucky ones. Most people are never going to die because they are never going to be born. The potential people who could have been here in my place but who will in fact never see the light of day outnumber the sand grains of Arabia."

Because life is so grand and easy to fall in love with, death is so horrible. But it is, nonetheless, only through the shear immense caliber of their opposites that death is so horrible, and life is so grand.

If you want an item at a store, there is a price you have to pay. When someone says, "I want to buy that," they don't actually mean they want to buy it. They want to have it. But they have to buy it in order to have it. Death is the price of living.

67

I don't believe in an afterlife. At least not in the traditional sense. I don't know where I came from or where I'm going. However, when I consider this lack of knowledge, how my entire ornate experience of life and self has come to form inside of me without any of my own desire or will for its inception, I acknowledge that there exists *something* beyond me that is equal part, if not wholly *me* that has and will continue to exist for as long as the universe does.

I am molecules of the universe that have become aware they are molecules, but I am no more or less important than any of the nearly infinite number of other molecules who have no idea what they are. And I am no more or less than the molecules who will never be *me* again.

There is an afterlife. And it comes after my life is over and I never exist again. What happens from there—wherever my quantum information and particles and whatever else go—is of as little concern and control to me as being born into this body and mind was to begin with. I think, if anything, this is actually the most pleasant way to think about all this. I feel a peace in it. A sense of connection. I am just another feature of the everything, swirling and vibrating. No more or less important than literally anything and everything else.

The feeling this gives me is not too dissimilar from the sensation I would graze once in a while when caught in a nearly perfect ray of sunlight or laid up next to a person in what felt like a nearly perfect moment or in a state of what seemed to be a nearly perfect chemical balance inside my brain. A visceral sense that everything is both meaningless and incomprehensibly meaningful at the same time. That the particularities and trivialities of myself and life are more or less meaningless, but that life itself, of which those particularities and trivialities are a part of, is of some cosmic everything.

This feeling would strike on any random, infrequent occasion and I would taste the eternity and ecstasy of the moment. And then the feeling would flee, often just as quick as it would come. But recently I have tasted it more and more frequently. And it's been leaving an indescribably rich and lovely aftertaste for longer and longer periods of time.

68

I think the times I've been most happy were when the notion of happiness never crossed my mind. At least no more than a fleeting, sensory, non-verbal realization of, "I feel happy right now."

To ask, "Am I happy?" answers the question with the question itself. If you have to ask, you almost certainly aren't. This goes for any iteration of such a question; "What is happiness?" or, "How can I be happy?" and so on. Whether or not these questions are even worth asking to begin with is beside the point. The point here is that if they are, to ask almost immediately implies the questions' undesired answers anyway.

Most of us know by now that happiness is not some achieved, constant thing at the end of any particular path. Of course, there are better and worse conditions of living, but after a certain point, happiness, like all states of mind, is only something to be experienced at times amidst a sea of other states. One doesn't need to do or know anything to be happy. How is a baby happy who knows nothing of happiness? It just is. Even here I am contradicting myself, though, by suggesting something that one might benefit from knowing in order to be it. But in truth, one does not need know this either. Perhaps at best it could only potentially help those needing the consideration that happiness needs no consideration, and by illuminating this paradox, one could theoretically opt out of it.

Like sadness, nostalgia, tiredness, excitement, hunger and all the rest, happiness comes and goes. To worship or try to cling to it does not stop it from coming and going. Worshiping the sun, which I nearly do, does not keep it from setting every night. And if my life's work was to stop the sun from setting, my life would've been an unending, horrible disappointment.

Now, during a time in which I have tried less and less to be or do or know anything related to happiness, I have found what seems to be an increased sense of it. Of course, I'm not happy all the time, but I'm happy when I'm happy. And I seem to be increasingly happy with that.

CHAPTER 10:
THE METAMORPHOSIS OF SELF

69

As the brain tumor grows, I can feel it more and more inside my skull. Between that and the treatments of the tumor, I've been feeling an increasing mix of head pain, deliriousness, drowsiness, highness, and surrealness. I feel like I am, in the most literal sense, losing my mind. The tumor is basically becoming as much my brain as my brain itself.

My mobility has been waning significantly as well. Fortunately, I have been able to maintain most control of my hands and arms, and I haven't been completely impaired in terms of independence. I have, however, been instructed by my doctor to start considering how I would potentially like to proceed once things get worse. In other words, how and where I want to die.

70

Over the past couple days, I've been reading some of my old work. I read two books that have always been my favorites. Then I read two that I've never really been that fond of after publishing. I've also been reading many of my old short stories; some of which I've never published and some spanning as far back as nearly twenty years. I also read one of the drafts of my first book that I wrote when I was in my early twenties.

There are words I wrote over ten years ago that almost seem to articulate how I feel right now better than I can right now. And at the same time, there are words in those same pieces that I can't even begin to resonate with. There is somehow both a former self I cringe at and don't know, and a former self that I envy and feel a tight proximity to at the same time.

It's a popular statement of belief to say that people change. Simultaneously, it seems equally popular to say that people don't. The truth, it seems, is that there's good reason for such a banal, impossible split. Because it's not really either. It's not an ever-changing self and it's not the same self. It's both together.

In terms of my *character*, there is some strange, central me that seems to have always been at the bottom of all the constantly changing versions of me, each expressing themselves a myriad of different ways, sometimes vastly different and contradicting, yet somehow all faced in the same direction and containing some consistent *sense* or *essence* that can't really be known or described on its own.

To fully know one's *character* or *self* would be like trying to know the entire *being* of a plot of land. One single plot of land will look, act, and serve completely different purposes over the span of its years, always having different things growing out of it and placed on it. And yet, it will always remain the same plot of land in terms of its physicality and basic features and resources. In other words, its *essence* will always be the same even though it will continually be something different on its surface.

As a result, one can't know the entire *being* of the plot of land by the *essence* of the plot alone, nor can one know it only by what exists on its surface for the same reason. However, furthermore, one cannot fully know or describe the plot of land by both it's land and what's on its surface at any single, given time either, because through time, that very same plot of land will look completely different and serve completely different purposes and expressions of itself. Thus, to know the entire plot of land is to know the combination of the land's *essence* and the expression of its surface multiplied by every phase of its existence across its lifetime, which will continue until it or the planet no longer exist at all.

Only when the land is gone can it be known fully. Which is to say that only once the self is gone can the self conclusively and comprehensively be known. This is, of course, impossible for the self to know of itself.

Moreover, even if it were possible, since we can't know why there is a plot of land at all and why plots of land fundamentally have any *essence* to begin with, one still wouldn't be able to truly know the plot of land (self) even after it had ended. The essential piece as to why and from where it exits would still be missing.

I've always known this sort of confusing observation of myself, often experienced as a nostalgia for the different components and qualities of each previous form of myself; a plot of land I could never return to even though I was always standing on the very same one. However, what's weird now is how little I even feel that much. I don't feel much of a nostalgia nor observational familiarity to myself.

I don't really recognize the voice in my previous writings as me. I resonate with some of the sentiments and ideas, but the words and voice seem more like different forms of a different person; someone else entirely.

It's commonly believed that our sense of self is merely our memories. That the present self is formed out of our ability to retain and live on the continual flow of remembering some amount of our past self. I think I agree with this, at least on the basic level. However, as my memory wanes and likely continues to a point of having nearly none at all, who will I be then? Will I no longer be myself? What will I be if I have no memories of myself if having no memories of myself absolves me from really having a *self*?

Will I finally be able to know myself once I no longer have one? What happens when you're still here, but there's no plot of land to stand on?

Like being drunk, high, or extremely tired, I feel weirdly sensitive to a lot of things that I wouldn't be otherwise. It's hard to focus on certain things, and hard to not focus on others. Specific details of things have a certain intrigue, while broader concepts feel kind of vague and hard to manage. I've felt increasingly confused, while increasingly detached from my own confusion, like I care less and less about the effects of my condition as it gets worse.

The process of dying is weird and confusing, but in most cases, I think the brain has an automated response hard-wired into it to prevent it from being too painful or too terrifying; almost as if the *programming system* of the brain still cared for its experiencer when configuring the death of itself.

Serious physical, deathly pain causes the body and mind to go into shock. Serious existential pain often causes the body and mind to go into denial, helpful grieving, cleverness, or humor. And slow loss of life often causes the mind to convince you you're okay by partly confusing the shit out of you and partly making it so you barely care anymore.

In truth, it's most likely that the hardwiring of the brain has these functions set up simply because they have survival merit. Shock, laughter, the feeling that it's going to be okay, and so on, all likely keep some percentage of people who would otherwise die or kill themselves from dying and killing themselves. And thus, these functions serve the sole evolutionary purpose of sustaining the brain.

Perhaps sometimes the system that the brain is formed on overlaps with the quality of the experience of it. This is both comforting in the sense that there seems to be some level of evolutionary concern for the quality of a conscious experience of it, but also incredibly terrifying in that such quality is likely determined by a system whose sole objective is to keep itself going for the sake of itself, and that it really has no genuine or empathetic care for the experiencer.

72

My memory has been increasingly fuzzy lately. Both long and short term. And moreover, I've been feeling really detached, almost as if I'm experiencing everything behind a glass pane. I think I've been hallucinating a little bit as well. I haven't brought that up to my doctors or anyone. Frankly, I wouldn't imagine there's much anyone could do. My doctor would likely prescribe more medications that cause more problems, and my mom and friends would just worry and that would cause more problems.

I realized how bad it's become earlier today. My mom asked me what I can only assume were some of the questions she always wanted to ask me, but only now felt compelled enough. I couldn't really recall anything she was referring to. The things she was asking about didn't register as memories. Even apparently really simple, obvious stuff. I had some vague, blurry conceptions, but based on her reactions to my attempts at answers, I wasn't really able to give her anything she was hoping for. I felt horrible. One, because I could tell how upset she was. I could see the devastation in her eyes as she fully realized how far gone I actually am. And two, because I fully realized it in that moment as well.

Even though I couldn't really answer her questions, I told her how much I loved and appreciated her. I could feel the sense that I had a reason to apologize, so I told her I was sorry too. Then I thanked her for being there.

I had similar conversations with some of my friends the past couple days as well. It's weird, of course, because it does make you wonder why you have to wait to say such things—to explicitly share those kinds of sentiments—until it's either too late or nearly too late.

73

I've been looking at the details of things a lot recently. Not just looking at them but almost being transfixed on them. As the reality of never being able to see or notice anything ever again approaches, the fascination with noticing every detail of everything seems to naturally grow.

I find myself lying on the couch, looking at each thread that creates the outer cover; each ever-so-slightly different in their particular color, arrangement, angle, and extrusion. I think about how many people were involved in designing, creating, and getting it to the point at which it's underneath me at that moment.

I find myself lying on the floor in the living room, looking at all the little nobs and nodes extruding out of the carpet like a simulated patch of grass that's perfectly designed to keep you cozy and comfortable without all the dirt and bugs.

I find myself noticing the texture and patterns of the curtains that drape down alongside my bed, thinking about how they've always been there but I've never appreciated how nice they make my room feel and how well their patterns sit against the incoming light.

I find myself following the dust particles that float around my head as fragmented sunbeams penetrate the cracks through the curtains. I wonder where each particle comes from and where they all go.

I've noticed these things before, but never like this. Never with such intensity to the point that it's almost surreal and meditative.

In these little moments, I almost feel okay.

I think I've realized with finality that the idea I considered my whole life—that in every attempt at comfort, solace, enjoyment, or connection; attempts that are almost always disguised by efforts of wealth, success, approval, status, and so on—all could be found just as easily in the minute, simple, and readily available objects and moments of ordinary life.

I think the wealth of life is found in everything or nothing.

Any moment of awareness and deep contemplation over the details of something as simple as a bug or a carpet or a chair or a tree or a pond and so on, is to experience the ultimate wealth of life. It's not that it must be something simple or free, but that it can just as easily be.

After a certain point, mostly everything is only as valuable as your perception of it. The noticing and caring of the details; the wondering, learning, and experiencing of the life that coats every object and moment. To feel and know this depth of life; to consider and question everything; to feel a oneness and intrigue spur out of the mere specs in the wood floor boards and bubbles in a pond; to try your best carry and rediscover the wonder of youthfulness throughout the whole of life. That is perhaps as good as it gets.

74

I have concluded mostly all treatments. I decided at this point that would be best. It wasn't really a hard decision. There is nothing much left to do other than eat pills and wait.

75

Dying reminds me of being a young child. A receding into helpless innocence.

No one has any memory without remembering it through who they are now, and thus, no memory can ever truly be trusted. But if I remember correctly, being a young child resembled this feeling. Just without the dying part. Sort of being babied and treated like you are responsible for very little, if not nothing. A helplessness and confusion that is both a nuisance and worthy of support.

I think we all have some longing to return to this state; a child-like innocence that is beyond blame and responsibility. Not necessarily innocent in action, but innocent in judgement. Innocent in judgment from others and judgment of one's self. There is a nirvana in this; a nirvana we all long for but can only seem to achieve when one is voided of mostly all self-agency.

76

With more pain has come more medications. And with more medications has come more strange side effects. I have continued to feel increasing delirium and sedateness, sometimes experiencing long states of unconsciousness as well as horrible waking pains and nausea. Recently, I've mostly just been in and out of extended periods of sleep with fragmented episodes of seemingly different realities scattered in between.

I've been on other psychotropic medications before, and I've gone through periods of consistent drug use in some form or another, so I've known the experience of having a sort of rhythmic sense of self that dips in and out of different states; various recurring peaks and lows that eventually become difficult to determine which one is more *you*. But I have certainly never felt it as extremely as I have in the last couple months. That's fairly obvious and to be expected, I suppose. But at times, I've genuinely felt like I've started to lose track of myself completely. I've lost track of my surroundings. Done the same thing over and over without realizing it. Confused strangers with my friends and my friends with strangers. Looked at my hands without recognizing them. Forgotten my own reflection. A complete depersonalization; sometimes beyond depersonalization, because it's almost as if there's no person or reality to even observe. I barely even know that anything's happening in these moments. It's closer to that of vaguely recalling a dream than experiencing a reality—if it can even be put into words.

And then sometimes I'll suddenly return to a stable state for a period of time as if nothing even happened. Or as if I were jumping in and out of familiar, but separate states of reality.

One of the weirdest parts is sleeping for full days or more at a time. And sometimes not even knowing or being able to wake myself up. More recently I've had to stay with my mom so she can monitor my sleep and help wake me up. Otherwise, I'd have to stay in the hospital or some assisted care type facility. Soon, I might have to no matter what.

A lot of the times when my mom wakes me up, I don't even recognize her, and it feels like I'm being woken up by a stranger.

To not recognize your own mom. Your own face. Your own life. At a certain point, it doesn't even matter where you live and die. Not necessarily in a bleak way, but perhaps in a freeing way.

You don't even care about not caring about what you don't care about anymore.

77

I can't really write much anymore. I've mostly been doing speech-to-text over the last few weeks, but I don't really want to do that much anymore either. I don't think much of what I've written recently is even discernable anyway. I've deleted most of it. I'll write a bunch when I'm in some state of delirium, thinking that I'm writing some incredible, otherworldly work of brilliance, barely aware of what I'm even saying. Then I'll read it back a day or two later when I'm a little more awake and realize how absolutely horrible it is. Mostly gibberish.

Some things don't change.

78

Being asleep most of the time is sort of like already being dead without actually losing a self to periodically return to. Sleeping in general is really just mini deaths throughout your entire life. It's a good deal, really. Scientifically, we don't really know why we sleep or why bad things happen to us if we don't. But recurring, mini death-like breaks from everything—that's enough of a reason for sleep for me.

During my life, I enjoyed sleeping. At least to some extent, if I remember correctly. I think there were likely moments where I even thought about how nice it would be to just sleep all day, all the time. Now, I sleep all day, all the time. And I would give anything to be awake all day, all the time.

79

Mostly everything I've ever known, ever been, ever believed, is all beginning to feel like an old TV show or movie that I used to love but haven't watched in a long time. A vague, distant, detached memory at best. Not even a show or film about me.

There's still a self here, writing this. But it's unclear exactly what's left of it. It has mostly let go of all that it is sure of. All of who it is and isn't. It's somewhere between here and not. Dream and awake. Dead and alive. It's strange, interesting, somewhat scary, and somewhat beautiful.

80

I have felt a disorientation over the past so many days or weeks that is so terrifyingly blissful. A helplessness that comes with a sense of freedom I have never felt or known before. Not a freedom in the sense that I can do whatever I want, but a freedom in the sense that, for the first time, I almost can't do anything I want. And soon, I literally won't be able to do anything I want at all. In this, I have become so majorly indifferent to everything that everything reveals a certain clarity and peacefulness I can't even begin to describe because it would only destroy the very essence of it.

Even in the abstract—even in the aesthetic—it would fall flat.

81

I would like this to be published. But if it isn't, that's okay too.

If it is, to anyone reading this, I have likely never known you and this is possibly the only time you have and will ever know me. A brief moment in both of our lives, disconnected in time and space. But perhaps we are more connected in this way than any other way possible. I will likely never know you, but if you have found any of yourself in what I've written, past or present, I have known you well.

82

I will be going to a hospice center at the end of the week. I will be spending any remaining time there. I have sort of past the point of my mom or anyone being able to properly take care of me at a house.

I don't know if I will be writing much more. I'm planning on bringing my laptop and I will try to write a little here and there if and when I can. I figure if I have anything still to say or write, I should get it on some page somewhere.

One never knows the last time they can.

Robert Pantano is the creator of the YouTube channel and production house known as Pursuit of Wonder, which covers similar topics of philosophy, science, and literature through short stories, guided experiences, video essays, and more.

Robert Pantano
youtube.com/pursuitofwonder
pursuitofwonder.com

Printed in Great Britain
by Amazon

65925941R00066